LEAD-UP
GAMES
TO
TEAM
SPORTS

O. William Blake
TEMPLE UNIVERSITY

Anne M. Volp
TEMPLE UNIVERSITY

ILLUSTRATIONS BY *Clover A. Morrissett*

Prentice-Hall, Inc.   ENGLEWOOD CLIFFS, N.J.

To those boys and girls
to whom we are indebted
for helping us learn how to teach

Current printing (last digit):

22 23 24 25

PRENTICE-HALL INTERNATIONAL, INC., *London*
PRENTICE-HALL OF AUSTRALIA, PTY., LTD., *Sydney*
PRENTICE-HALL OF CANADA, LTD., *Toronto*
PRENTICE-HALL OF INDIA (PRIVATE) LIMITED, *New Delhi*
PRENTICE-HALL OF JAPAN, INC., *Tokyo*

PREFACE

This book is a single source of good games "leading up" to team sports. Challenging games are the stock-in-trade of every successful physical education teacher and recreation leader. Every physical education teacher sooner or later feels the need for new and different games that will enrich, vary, and vitalize his program. These games are the means through which many of the objectives of physical education are achieved. Without them physical education programs can become dull and meaningless to students.

Books written on team sports are geared usually for either boys or girls. In this book the lead-up games have been presented so that they are applicable to both boys' and girls' programs.

Lead-up games to basketball, field hockey, lacrosse, soccer, softball, speedball, speed-a-way, touch football, and volleyball have been selected, since these team games: (1) are the nucleus of most physical education and recreation programs; (2) are highly organized and lend themselves to the lead-up game approach; (3) cover a wide range of interest of both boys and girls; (4) appeal to boys and girls when their interest in team games is strongest; and (5) utilize the equipment and facilities most often available.

These lead-up games can be used effectively from the third grade, when interest in team games begins, through high school. The games are arranged progressively from the simplest to the most complex to aid the inexperienced teacher in developing a program and, at the same time, to provide new ideas for the experienced teacher.

The lead-up games are easy to understand and adaptable to the local situation. The teacher will have no difficulty in determining the skills and number of players involved, the equipment and space needed, and the method of scoring. Effective variations of the game can also be readily discovered. The number of players suggested for each game is merely a guide to provide the greatest enjoyment and maximum activity for the students. The description of the game itself indicates the equipment needed and whether a game is appropriate for the playfield, playground, gymnasium, or campsite.

Fundamental skills are not analyzed in this book since there are many sources available in which analyses are presented. Our emphasis is on lead-up games in which fundamental skills and game strategy may be practiced and developed.

In studying this symposium of lead-up games, the teacher will discover a pattern to aid him in creating his own lead-up games. It is our hope that it will stimulate many to develop additional lead-up games that can be shared with others.

We wish to express our appreciation to Helen Christian, Jane Vache, and Elizabeth Williams for reading portions of the manuscript and suggesting improvements.

O. W. B.
A. M. V.

CONTENTS

Soccer—Speedball, Speed-A-Way

Softball

Touch Football

Volleyball

LEAD-UP GAMES
A Game Way to Sports

Let the main objective of this, our didactic be as follows:
To seek and find a method of instruction, by which teachers
may teach less, and learners learn more . . .

JOHN AMOS COMENIUS
1592–1670

The lead-up approach to teaching team sports is a method of instruction, by which learners learn more, learn faster, and with greater interest and understanding. Lead-up games * may be defined as modified team games that involve one or more of the fundamental skills, rules, and procedures used in a major team game. Such modified games start with simple activities involving a few skills and lead to more complex activities involving several techniques. This is an educational method that is sound in theory and effective in practice.

Values of Lead-up Games

Learning. Anyone who has worked with boys and girls knows that as far as most students are concerned, "The game is the thing." They don't want to practice isolated skills; they want to play the game.

Few students are sufficiently interested in improving their skills in team games to want to spend much time on formal drills. Most boys and girls are much more interested in learning as they play. If, therefore, skills can be practiced through challenging lead-up games, a high level of interest will be maintained. Interest is basic to learning. Lead-up games help the learner build a picture of the total activity by providing performance in the whole activity or a relatively large whole-part. This makes practice purposeful and interesting to students.

---

* There are those who object to the idea of lead-up games on the basis that the games are only a means to the more highly organized team game. We feel, however, that lead-up games can be both means and ends: they can be ends in themselves by providing some students with a less complex game suited to their skill level. For these students the lead-up game could well be the final or end game.

1

Lead-up games in no way minimize the need for drills. By combining games and drills a most effective learning experience is provided. In fact, students, after having participated in lead-up games, develop an even keener interest in practicing and perfecting the skills, for they are better able to see how isolated skills relate to a game situation.

Progression. Lead-up games can provide a progression from simple to complex that is educationally sound. One of the criticisms most frequently leveled at physical education is lack of progression in the program. In the days of formal gymnastics progression was the keynote, but today in many game-oriented physical education programs this emphasis is lacking. Physical education programs must provide progression, sequence, and continuity if they are to be educationally acceptable. Lead-up games can be selected with this developmental approach in mind.

Team Play. A basic need of boys and girls is to be an accepted member of a group. Team games provide one such opportunity to meet this basic need. Unfortunately not all boys and girls can be members of interscholastic and intramural teams. However, lead-up games provide an opportunity for *all* boys and girls, regardless of ability, to be members of a team and to work cooperatively toward its success. It should be the birthright of every growing boy and girl to be a contributing member of a team.

Some teachers and leaders, in attempting to recognize this interest of students in team games, have thrown them a ball and allowed the students to play with little direction and with almost no teaching of fundamental skills. This approach is unfortunate, for it has given physical education an unfavorable image. A skillful and resourceful teacher, however, with a number of progressively organized lead-up games can utilize this consuming interest of boys and girls to provide an excellent learning situation.

Competition. Constructive competition has no counterpart in stimulating learning. But competition for what purpose? Competition not to *prove*, but to *improve*.

Competition will bring out the best in a person when it is correctly approached. Leaders and teachers must equate opponents in such a way that the outcome is never certain until the final whistle is blown. Under ideal competitive conditions learning flourishes.

Team competition should be included as a part of the regular physical education class program and should not be restricted to after school intramural programs. If only fundamental drills were taught during the class period, many of the students would never have an opportunity to participate on a team or to utilize the fundamentals learned, since not all students in a school participate on an intramural team. Lead-up games during class time provide a means for this team competition.

Content. The growing trend toward organizing physical education by units, such as basketball, soccer, and volleyball, gives support to the need for lead-up games to give added content to these units. Many programs in physical education are too narrow in scope. Units of instruction are too limited in content. A wider selection of challenging experiences is needed to stimulate and facilitate learning. Lead-up games should be a basic and integral part of every resource unit developed for a team sport.

Activity. The President's Council on Physical Fitness has recommended that a minimum of fifteen minutes of each daily physical education period be devoted to vigorous physical activity. Properly selected and organized lead-up games can provide maximum participation in such vigorous activity.

Adaptability. The challenge of physical education is to provide a flexible program that is adaptable to *all* students. Many programs, unfortunately, are geared to the highly skilled student. Lead-up games provide an opportunity for the less skilled to play a less difficult game. This can be as satisfying for them as the game in its most complex form is for the more gifted student. Lead-up games of varying degrees of difficulty may be conducted simultaneously to meet these individual differences.

Another major problem in any physical education program is getting all students to share in the game experience. This is particularly true where large classes are found. Highly organized team games do not always accommodate a large number of players. Basketball is a good example. There are lead-up games to basketball, however, that will utilize many more players than the game of basketball itself.

Lead-up games also aid in solving the problem of inadequate space because they can be modified, adjusted, and adapted to fit the available area.

Principles for the Selection and Use of Lead-up Games

These basic principles should govern the selection and use of lead-up games:

1. Lead-up games should be presented in order, from simple to more complex.
2. Lead-up games should be used to complement drills and not replace them.
3. Lead-up games should be organized to provide maximum participation.
4. Lead-up games should provide evenly matched competition.
5. Lead-up games and the necessary equipment should be suited to the ability of the players.

6. Lead-up games should utilize as much equipment as feasible to provide maximum activity and participation.
7. Lead-up games should be adapted to make maximum use of the space and time available.
8. Lead-up games should have a standardized rotation plan whereby all players are given an opportunity to play all positions.
9. Lead-up games should be adapted and modified in whatever ways necessary to meet the needs and abilities of the boys and girls as well as the objectives of the program.
10. Lead-up games should be planned so as to contribute to the growth and development of boys and girls.

Lead-up games are not a panacea for all the problems involved in teaching highly organized team sports, but they do present one more educational method that can be extremely effective in the plans of a resourceful teacher. In the final analysis the lead-up game approach is only as effective as the teacher's understanding of it.

Safety Suggestions for Lead-up Games

Safety is not an accident. Every teacher has a moral and legal responsibility to protect his students. Some safety suggestions concerning lead-up games are:

1. Discuss and emphasize safety practices and precautions with the class upon introducing a new lead-up game.
2. Provide some practice of the skills involved before playing the game, for skilled players are less prone to accidents than the unskilled.
3. Provide proper supervision for all activities at all times.
4. Insure an adequate warm-up period prior to participation in lead-up games.
5. Divide students into groups of comparable ability before playing a lead-up game.
6. Prevent fatigue by slowly working into lead-up games involving endurance.
7. Arrange playing areas so there is ample space between games and fences or walls.
8. Remove objects and obstacles from the playing area.
9. Require all students to wear gymnasium shoes.
10. Have those students who wear glasses wear glass guards.
11. Prevent unnecessary roughness.
12. Use a partially deflated ball when the object of the game is to hit a person with a ball.

BASKETBALL

Lead-up Games Designed to Develop Basketball Skills

Lead-up games	Basic skills involved				
	Passing	Catching	Guarding	Dribbling	Shooting
Bombardment	X	X			
Guard ball	X	X	X		
Team pin guard	X	X	X		
Bull in the ring	X	X	X		
Circle target	X	X	X		
Circle pole ball	X	X	X		
End ball	X	X			
Dribble contest				X	
Basketball relay	X	X		X	X
Team twenty-one					X
Around the world					X
Basket baseball	X	X			X
Keep away	X	X	X		
Fast break	X	X	X	X	
Field ball	X	X	X		
Captain ball	X	X	X		
Nine-court basketball	X	X	X		X
Target ball	X	X	X	X	
Net basketball	X	X	X		X
Sideline basketball	X	X	X		X
Half-court basketball	X	X	X	X	X

Players	8 to 10 on a team. Teams unlimited.
Equipment	Basketballs and 6 or more Indian clubs.
Area	Gymnasium or playground. (40 by 60 feet)
Skills	Throwing, catching, and hitting a fixed target.
Game	The object is to knock down as many of the opponent's clubs as possible. Each team has several balls. Players may throw the balls at the clubs from anywhere in their own half of the court. Opposing players may catch the balls or block them with any part of their bodies.
Scoring	The team knocking down the most clubs in the designated time is the winner.
Variations	(1) Specify the kind of pass to be used. (2) Use different kinds of balls.

40' x 60'

GUARD BALL

Players	8 to 10 on a team. Teams unlimited.
Equipment	Basketballs.
Area	Gymnasium or playground. (20 feet between lines)
Skills	Passing, catching, and guarding.
Game	The object is for players on the team outside the boundaries to pass the ball back and forth between the players in the center. The players in the center block the ball as they would if they were guards in basketball. A ball thrown above the height of the players does not count. After 3 minutes the teams change positions.
Scoring	One point is scored each time the ball is passed successfully below head level between the center players.
Variations	(1) Specify the kind of pass to be used. (2) Use several balls.

20'

TEAM PIN GUARD

Players   8 to 10 on a team. Teams unlimited.

Equipment   Basketballs and 1 Indian club for each team.

Area   Gymnasium or playground.

Skills   Passing and guarding.

Game   Each team forms a circle. The object is to knock down an Indian club in the center of the circle with a basketball. One player from the opposing team is inside each circle for the purpose of protecting the club. Players throw the balls at the club and attempt to knock it down while the guard defends the club with his hands, legs, and body. Players may retrieve a ball inside the circle but must return to the edge of the circle to throw. After each score the guards return to their teams and new guards are chosen.

Scoring   One point is scored by the team that knocks down the club first.

Variations   (1) Use more than one guard. (2) Use several balls.

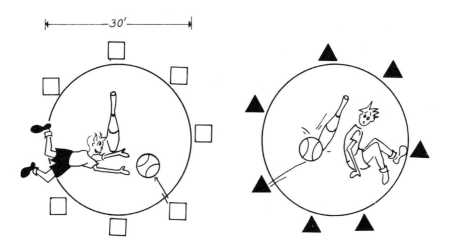

BULL IN THE RING

Players 8 to 10 on a team. Teams unlimited.

Equipment Basketballs.

Area Gymnasium or playground.

Skills Passing, catching, and guarding.

Game The object is to see which team's defensive man can intercept or tie up the other team's ball first. The teams, who have each formed a circle, pass the ball back and forth and attempt to keep it away from the bull, a player of the opposing team who stands in the center. No player may pass directly to the neighbor on his right or left. No player may hold the ball longer than 3 seconds. Any pass is permissible except the lob pass. As soon as the ball is tied up or intercepted by a bull, new center players take over.

Scoring One point is scored by the team whose bull first intercepts or ties up the ball.

Variations (1) Specify the kind of pass to be used. (2) Use several bulls.

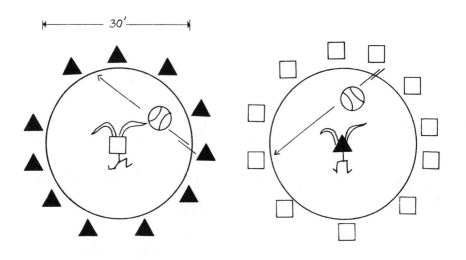

Players	8 to 10 on a team. Teams unlimited.
Equipment	Basketball.
Area	Gymnasium or playground.
Skills	Passing, catching, and guarding.
Game	The object is for one team outside the large circle to pass the ball to a teammate in the inner circle who is surrounded by opponents. All throws must be made while the throwers are outside of their circle. The defensive team may bat or kick the ball away, but they may not catch it. After 3 minutes the teams exchange positions.
Scoring	One point is scored each time a pass is completed to the center player.
Variations	Use several balls.

CIRCLE POLE BALL

Players 8 to 10 on a team. Teams unlimited.

Equipment Basketball and jump standard.

Area Gymnasium or playground. (Inside circle 20 feet in diameter, outside circle 30 feet in diameter)

Skills Passing, catching, and hitting a fixed target.

Game Half the players on each team are forwards and half are guards. The object is for a forward, who is outside the circle, to hit the pole with the ball. Guards, inside the circle, try to prevent forwards of the opposing team from hitting the pole. The game starts by a jump ball between two guards at the center line. The guard who secures the ball passes it to one of his forwards, who may try to hit the pole himself or may pass to another forward. After each score, guards and forwards exchange positions.

Scoring One point is scored each time the ball hits the pole.

Variations Use several balls.

30′

END BALL

Players	8 to 10 on a team. Teams unlimited.
Equipment	Basketballs.
Area	Gymnasium or playground. (40 by 60 feet)
Skills	Passing and catching.
Game	Three or four of the players of each team are selected as end-zone players. The object is for each team to throw the ball to one of its end-zone players. The game starts with an end-zone player of each team in possession of a ball. This player tries to throw the ball to one of his fielders. Fielders of both teams try to secure the ball and throw it to one of their end men, who must catch the ball on the fly without leaving the end zone. After every 5 points the end-zone players rotate with the fielders.
Scoring	One point is scored for each successful throw by a fielder to an end-zone player.
Variations	(1) Use several balls. (2) Start with either a jump ball or a throw-in from the sideline. (3) Have the end-zone players shoot for a basket from the spot where the ball is caught (2 points for each basket made).

DRIBBLE CONTEST

Players	6 to 8 on a team. Teams unlimited.
Equipment	Basketballs.
Area	Gymnasium or playground.
Skills	Dribbling.
Game	The object is for one team to complete the dribble course first. A ball is given the player at one end of each line (diagonally opposite). On a signal each player dribbles to his left all the way around the rectangle formed by the two teams. When he reaches his starting point he hands the ball to the next player, who dribbles around the rectangle.
Scoring	The team that gets back to its starting position first is the winner.
Variations	(1) Have players dribble with their weak hand. (2) Have them dribble in the opposite direction (to their right). (3) Have them weave in and out between players of both teams.

Players	8 to 10 on a team. Teams unlimited.
Equipment	2 basketballs and goals.
Area	Gymnasium or playground. (35- by 60-foot court)
Skills	Passing, catching, and shooting.
Game	The object is for the player whose number is called to pass the ball to each one of his teammates, try for a basket, and return the ball to the starting position before his opponent. At the start two basketballs are placed on the floor midway between the two lines of players. Each player has a number. When his number is called, he runs to get one ball and begins passing it from the middle of the floor to each teammate. When the player has thrown to each teammate, he dribbles to the basket and takes one shot. The player then recovers the shot and dribbles to the center of the court where he places the ball down.
Scoring	Two points are scored for the player finished first, and 2 more are scored if a basket is made.
Variations	(1) Specify the kind of pass to be used or shot to be made. (2) Have the player shoot until he makes a basket.

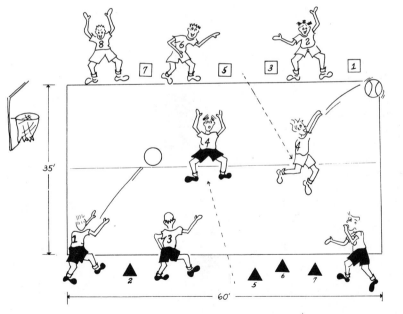

TEAM TWENTY-ONE

Players	6 to 8 on a team. Teams unlimited.
Equipment	Basketballs and goals.
Area	Gymnasium or playground.
Skills	Shooting.
Game	The object is to see how many team members can score 21 points by shooting baskets. Each team member is permitted a long shot and a follow-up shot. The long shot is taken anywhere from behind the extended free-throw line. The follow-up shot is taken from the spot where the ball is recovered after the long shot. A player continues to shoot as long as he makes both a long and short shot in succession. Each team participates at its own basket.
Scoring	Two points for a long shot and 1 for a short one. Total each individual member's score. The team scoring the most points wins.
Variations	Specify various kinds of shots, for example, jump shot.

15'

Players	6 to 8 on a team. Teams unlimited.
Equipment	Basketballs and goals.
Area	Gymnasium or playground.
Skills	Shooting.
Game	The object is to see which team can have the most members make baskets from all the designated spots. Each team member begins at the first spot and continues as long as he makes the shot. When he misses, he has two choices. The first is to wait for his next turn and continue from the place where he missed. The second is to "risk it," which means that he gets another shot from where he missed. If he makes this, he continues. If he misses, he starts over from the beginning on his next turn. If a player finishes, he starts over again. Each team participates at its own basket.
Scoring	The team completing the most circuits is the winner.
Variations	If one player overtakes another at a spot, the one who has been there longest must return to the first position.

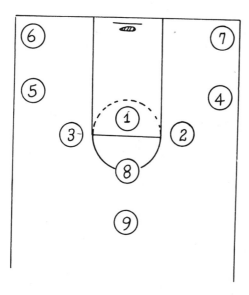

BASKET BASEBALL

Players	8 to 10 on a team. Teams unlimited.
Equipment	Basketball and goal.
Area	Gymnasium or playground. (35-foot bases)
Skills	Passing, catching, and shooting.
Game	The object is for the batting team to make runs and the fielding team to put its opponents out by shooting baskets. Each person has a number. Number 1 of the batting team throws the ball from the home plate as far into the field as possible and runs the bases without stopping. Meanwhile, number 1 on the fielding team positions himself near the basketball goal. As soon as his teammates recover the ball, they relay it to him. He in turn attempts to shoot a basket. If he can make a basket before the batter gets home, the batter is out. If the batter gets home before a basket is made, he scores a run for his team. Then the number 2's go, and so on. After everyone has batted, teams change sides.
Scoring	One point is scored for each run made.
Variations	(1) Specify the kind of shot. (2) Have the runners make more than one circuit of the bases. (3) Have the batter place kick, drop kick, or punt a soccer ball or serve a volleyball. (4) Have the fielders make a set number of passes before they may pass to the shooter.

Players	8 to 10 on a team. Teams unlimited.
Equipment	Basketball.
Area	Gymnasium or playground. (40 by 60 feet)
Skills	Passing, catching, and guarding.
Game	The object is for one team to keep the ball away from the opponents while passing to teammates. The player with the ball may not walk with it or dribble. No player on defense is allowed to make personal contact with the player in possession of the ball, but the ball may be knocked down or intercepted when passed. Guarding is the same as in basketball.
Scoring	Score is determined by either the length of time a team can keep possession of the ball or the number of completed passes made in succession.
Variations	(1) Use several balls. (2) Allow dribbling.

40' X 60'

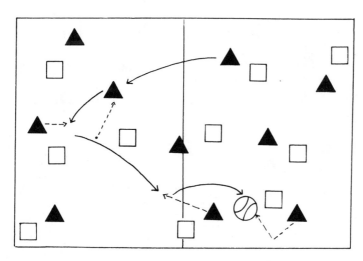

FAST BREAK

Players 8 to 10 on a team. Teams unlimited.

Equipment Basketball.

Area Gymnasium or playground. (40 by 60 feet)

Skills Passing, catching, dribbling, and guarding.

Game The object is for members of the team at one end to pass the ball to their teammates on the other side of the neutral zone. No one is allowed in the neutral zone. Basketball rules are in effect. Opposing team members try to knock down the ball or intercept it before it can be caught.

Scoring One point is scored for each successful pass across the neutral zone.

Variations (1) Use more than one ball. (2) Widen the neutral zone.

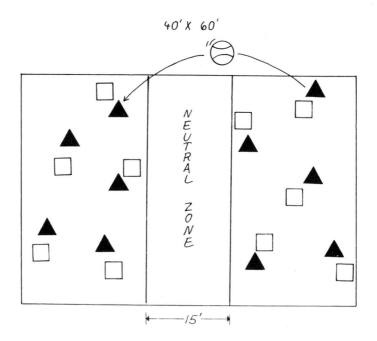

Players	8 to 10 on a team. Teams unlimited.
Equipment	Basketball.
Area	Playground or gymnasium. (30 by 60 yards)
Skills	Passing, catching, and guarding.
Game	The object is to advance the ball by throwing it and to score by passing the ball through a soccer goal. The method of play resembles soccer in form, but the handling of the ball is more similar to that in basketball. The game starts with a throw-off by one team from the center of the field, with the ball going at least 5 yards into the opponent's half of the field. The ball may not be handed to a teammate; it must be thrown or bounced. A player catching the ball or picking it up cannot walk with the ball and must throw it within 3 seconds. The goalie may run with the ball in the penalty area. Guarding is permitted as in basketball.
Scoring	One point for a goal made from within the penalty area and 2 points for a goal made from outside the penalty area.
Variations	Allow dribbling.

30' X 60' YARDS

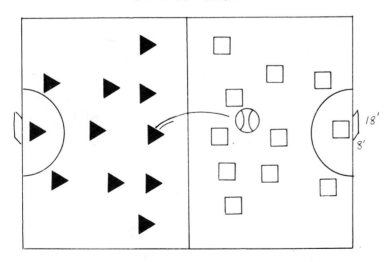

18'

8'

CAPTAIN BALL

Players   8 to 10 on a team. Teams unlimited.

Equipment   Basketball.

Area   Gymnasium or playground. (40 by 60 feet)

Skills   Passing, catching, and guarding.

Game   The object is for the players on base, or forwards, to throw the ball to their captain. The game is started at center court by a jump ball between two guards. The guards attempt to throw the ball to their forwards on base. The forwards are the only players who can throw directly to the captain. The two base players farthest from each other are the captains. Forwards may have one foot off their base but never both feet. The guards may not step on the base or contact the forwards. No player may run with the ball or hold it longer than 3 seconds. Guards and forwards change after each score.

Scoring   One point is scored each time a captain receives the ball from one of the forwards.

Variations   Captain basketball, a variation in which only the captains are confined to a base. Guards and forwards are restricted to their half of the court; otherwise it is played like basketball.

40' X 60'

NINE-COURT BASKETBALL

Players	9 on a team. Teams unlimited.
Equipment	Basketball and goals.
Area	Gymnasium or playground. (40 by 60 feet)
Skills	Passing, catching, guarding, and shooting.
Game	The object is for the forwards in the three courts closest to each basket to score. A player from each team plays in each court. The game starts with a center jump in court 9. Players may not step out of their court. After each goal made, players rotate to the next higher numbered court. Number 9 goes to number 1. There is no dribbling; otherwise, basketball rules apply. After each basket, play is resumed by a center jump in court 9.
Scoring	Two points are scored for each basket made.
Variations	(1) More courts or fewer courts can be used depending on the number of players. (2) Allow dribbling within the court.

40' X 60'

TARGET BALL

Players 8 to 10 on a team. Teams unlimited.

Equipment Basketball.

Area Gymnasium or playground. (40 by 60 feet)

Skills Catching, passing, dribbling, and guarding.

Game One player from each team is designated as a target player. The object is to score by using the ball to tag the opponent's target player. Basketball rules govern the game; players may pass, dribble, or use a basketball manuever to tag the opponent's target player with the ball. Target players may tag a target player of the other team. Following a score, the team scored against puts the ball in play with an out-of-bounds throw nearest to the point where the score was made.

Scoring One point is scored each time a target player is tagged by the ball.

Variations (1) Restrict the target player to an area. (2) The target player cannot run, but must walk or hop to avoid being tagged.

40' X 60'

Players 8 to 10 on a team. Teams unlimited.

Equipment Basketball, net, and goals.

Area Gymnasium or playground. (40 by 60 feet)

Skills Catching, passing, guarding, and shooting.

Game The object is to advance the ball to the team member who is in the keyhole so that he can shoot for the basket. The ball is tossed back and forth over the net in order to reach the player within the keyhole. The keyhole is the only area from which a try for a basket may be made. The game starts by a center jump at midcourt. Players are not allowed to dribble; otherwise basketball rules apply. After each basket a new keyhole player is selected.

Scoring Two points are scored each time a basket is made.

Variations Have the teams line up and number off by fours on opposite sidelines. One member of each team is in the keyhole. Call a number and throw the ball against the backboard. Those with the number called run onto the court to get the ball and attempt to get it to their keyhole player. After a basket is scored, players return to their places and a new number is called.

40' X 60'

SIDELINE BASKETBALL

Players Any number. No more than 10 on the court at one time.

Equipment Basketball and goals.

Area Gymnasium or playground. (40 by 60 feet)

Skills All the skills of basketball except dribbling.

Game The object is to score as in basketball. Each team is lined up and numbered off along opposite sidelines. The first five players from each team come onto the court. The game is played like regulation basketball, with the exception that no player within the court may pass directly to another court player but must each time pass to a sideline player. This rule does not apply to successive attempts to make a goal. The ball may not be dribbled. Sideline players must stay off the court. Following each score, two new teams of five players each take the court with the former players retiring to the sidelines.

Scoring Two points are scored each time a basket is made.

Variations Have each sideline team number off by fours. Call a number and throw the ball against the backboard. Those with the number called run to get the ball and play using the sideline players until a basket is made.

40' X 60'

Players   4 to 6 on a team. Teams unlimited.

Equipment   Basketball and goal.

Area   Gymnasium or playground. (30 by 40 feet)

Skills   All the skills of basketball.

Game   The object is to score as in basketball, using only one-half court. Both teams shoot for the same basket. The game is played like basketball with this exception: if a ball changes hands, the team gaining possession must take the ball behind the extended free-throw line before the ball can be worked in for a shot at the goal.

Scoring   Two points are scored for each field goal made and 1 point for a free throw.

Variations   The team scoring keeps possession of the ball.

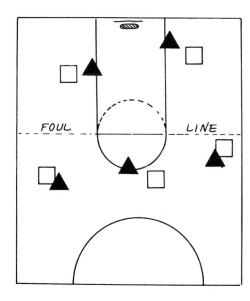

30' X 40'

FOUL   LINE

The following lead-up games, found elsewhere in this book, can easily be used to lead up to basketball by substituting a basketball and the basketball skills one wishes to develop.

Around the Clock	38	Mickey Mouse	92
Around the Horn	118	Newcomb	164
Attack	82	Obstacle Dribble	37
Catch, Go, and Throw	78	On the Whistle	61
Circle Pass	71	Over and Under	137
Count Off	70	Scat	64
Covering	55	Star Lacrosse	72
Diagonal Shuttle	46	Steal the Football	142
Dodging and Tackling	42	Target Pitch	119
Hit the Ball	147	Teacher Ball	93
Hit and Stop	33	Twist	62
Interception	81	Wall Rebound	63
Leader Ball	168	Zig-Zag Throw	117
Long Pass	65		

FIELD HOCKEY

Lead-up Games Designed to Develop Field Hockey Skills

Lead-up games	Dribbling	Driving	Fielding	Dodging	Tackling	Push passing	Bullying	Scooping	Rolling-in	Shooting	Marking	Covering	Rules
Nobbies							X						X
Hit and stop		X	X										
Hit away	X	X											
Circle dribble	X												
Triangles		X	X			X							
Obstacle dribble	X												
Around the clock	X		X			X							
Dodge around objects	X	X	X	X	X								
End-zone hockey	X	X	X	X	X	X	X						X
Dodging and tackling		X	X	X	X								
Scoop	X	X						X					
Bully	X	X					X						X
Goals	X	X	X	X	X								X
Diagonal shuttle	X	X	X										
Flicks						X							
Alley ball									X				X
Shooting goals	X	X	X							X			X
Two-man figure eight	X		X	X		X							
Halfbacks attack	X	X	X	X	X	X				X	X		X
Corner goals			X	X	X	X		X		X	X		X
Covering	X	X	X	X	X	X							
Lane hockey	X	X	X	X	X	X		X	X		X	X	X

NOBBIES

Players   8 to 24.

Equipment   Sticks or wand, and nobbies. Suggestion: nobbies may be made with 2 rubber balls fastened with a leather thong.

Area   Gymnasium or playing field. (50 by 100 yards)

Skills   Bullying, positions, beginning rules of field hockey, offensive and defensive strategy.

Game   The object of the game is to throw the nobbies, by using the stick, over the opponent's goal line. Divide players into equal teams. Give each team a different colored shirt or pinnie. Place nobbies in the center of the field. The teams' centers stand facing each other, with their left sides toward their goals and with the nobbies between them. On referee's whistle the centers bully, by alternately hitting the ground and opponent's stick three times. After the third hit of the sticks they quickly try to scoop up the nobbies to their goals. After the nobbies have been put into play, all players on the field are eligible to scoop up the nobbies with their sticks and throw them or run with them. Game is played in quarters of 8 to 10 minutes.

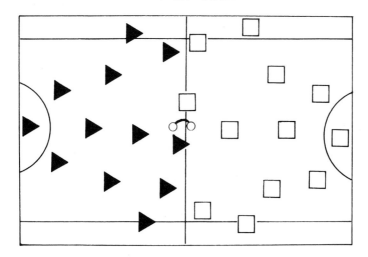

50 X 100 YARDS

FOULS: Tripping, shoving with the hand or body, striking a person with a stick.

PENALTIES: Free throw with all players 5 yards away.

OUT-OF-BOUNDS: When the nobbies pass wholly over the sideline, a player of the team not responsible for the out-of-bounds throws them into the field. Out-of-bounds play cannot be thrown over the goal line.

Scoring   One point is scored each time the nobbies go over the goal line.

Variations   Hand hockey indoors using volleyball.

HIT AND STOP

Players Unlimited. Two straight lines 10 yards apart; players opposite one another are partners.

Equipment Hockey sticks, balls, and a stopwatch.

Area Playing field.

Skills Driving (stressing quick wrist action), speed, and footwork.

Game The object of the game is to score the greatest number of hits in 1 minute. On signal, line 1 hits the ball to line 2, making certain the ball is on the stick side. Player 2 stops the ball, and hits back to player 1 on the stick side. Continue for 1 minute.

Scoring Each hit counts 1 point. The couple with the highest score goes to the head of the line; the others follow according to their scores. Repeat several times to encourage the players to reach and maintain a position at the top of the line. As skill develops the lines may be moved farther apart.

Variations Substitute push pass, scoop, or flick for the drive.

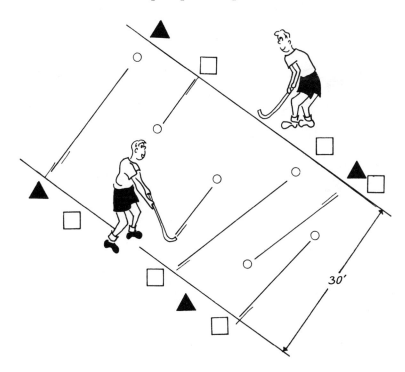

HIT AWAY

Players   Unlimited. Any number of equal lines.

Equipment   Hockey sticks and balls.

Area   Playing field.

Skills   Dribbling and driving on the run.

Game   The object of the game is to hit the ball a long distance. The first two players in each line have a ball. On signal, the first player in each line dribbles the ball to the 5-yard line, drives the ball ahead hard, and follows the ball immediately to the spot where it has stopped. Five points are awarded to the team whose player has hit the ball the farthest, 4 for second place, 3 for third, 2 for fourth, and 1 for fifth. On signal, the second player in line takes a turn, hitting the ball on the run. The first player returns the ball to player 3. Each line keeps its own score.

Scoring   The highest sum total of points is the winner.

Variations   Push pass may be substituted for the drive.

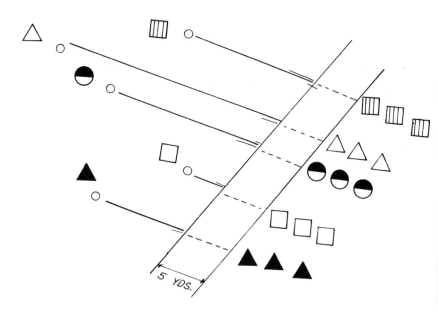

5 YDS.

Players	Circle formation. 8 to each circle is a desirable number.
Equipment	Hockey sticks and balls.
Area	Playing field.
Skills	Dribbling, controlling ball, and footwork.
Game	The object of the game is to dribble around the outside of the circle and return to original position rapidly. Form two or more circles, each representing a team. On a signal, the first player on each team starts to dribble on the outside of the circle, returns to his original position, and passes the ball to the player on his right. The first team to finish is declared the winner.
Scoring	Five points for first place, 4 for second, 3 for third-place finishers.
Variations	Players may dribble in and out through the spaces in the circle. Stress keeping the ball in front of the right foot. Players should shift the feet rather than the ball to accomplish this.

TRIANGLES

Players	Unlimited.
Equipment	Hockey sticks and balls.
Area	Playing field or gymnasium.
Skills	Fielding from the left and right, footwork, passing left and right, push passing, right and left driving.
Game	The object of the game is to hit and field the ball as many times as possible in a given time limit. Example: hit counterclockwise for 1 minute, then clockwise the next.
Scoring	The groups with the highest score at the end of each game score 5 points for first place, 3 points for second place, and 1 point for third place. The team with the highest total number of points wins the game.
Variations	(1) One defensive player in the center of the triangle may attempt to intercept the ball. (2) Use of various strokes.

Players   8 to 10 on a team. Unlimited.

Equipment   Hockey sticks, balls, and 3, 5, or 7 obstacles. (Note: students, pinnies, or boxes may be used as obstacles.)

Area   Playing field or gymnasium. (Balls should be covered for indoor use to prevent loss of control.)

Skills   Dribbling, controlling ball, footwork.

Game   The object of the game is to dribble around the obstacles as quickly as possible. Each team stands in file formation behind the starting line. The obstacles are placed in line with each team, 20 feet from the starting line and 5 yards apart. On signal "Go" first player in each team dribbles the ball toward the obstacles, and, going to left of first obstacle, weaves through them up and back to the starting line. As soon as the first player crosses the starting line, the next player takes his turn. The first team returning to its original position is the winner.

Variations   (1) Several games may be played with 5 points for first place, 4 points for second place, 3 points for third place, and so on. The team with the greatest number of points at the end of playing time is the winner. (2) Substitute for dribble stick-side dodge, non stick-side dodge, or scoop.

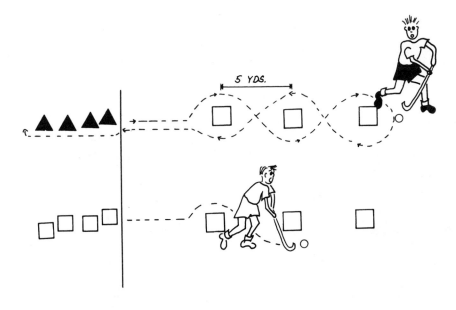

5 YDS.

AROUND THE CLOCK

Players Unlimited. 8 to 10 on a team.

Equipment Hockey sticks and balls.

Area Gymnasium or playing field.

Skills Push passing, fielding, footwork.

Game The object of the game is for each team to execute the skills with accuracy and attempt to complete the game as rapidly as possible. The players stand in a circle, with 3 to 5 feet between each two players; one player stands in the center of the circle with a ball. The center player pushes the ball to a player on the circle, who fields the ball, and immediately pushes it back to the center. The center pushes the ball to the next player on the right of the circle. When the ball has been passed to each player in the circle, the second player takes the center position. The game is repeated until each player has had an opportunity in the center position.

Scoring The team that finishes first is the winner. When several teams are competing, a 5-3-1 point system may be used.

Variations Each illustration shows a different method of playing the same game.

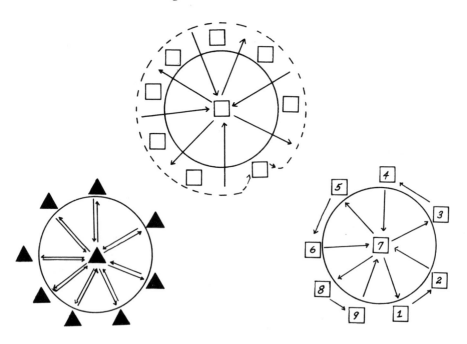

Players	8 to 10 on a team. Unlimited.
Equipment	Hockey sticks, balls, and 3 objects for each participating team.
Area	Playing field or gymnasium.
Skills	Dribbling, stick-side dodging, non stick-side dodging, circular tackling, driving, and fielding.
Game	The object of the game is for each line to finish first. Each team forms a line behind the starting line. The objects are placed in line with each team, 30 feet from the starting line and 5 yards apart. On signal the first player on each team dribbles the ball toward the objects; a stick-side dodge is executed around the first object, a non stick-side dodge around the second object, a circular tackle movement (right shoulder) around the third object. The player then drives the ball-back to the next player in line. A team is disqualified if a player moves across the starting line to receive a ball. If the ball comes to a complete stop before crossing the line, the player may move ahead to play it.
Scoring	The first team to return to its original position is the winner.
Variations	None.

OBSTACLES — 5 YARDS APART

END-ZONE HOCKEY

Players	6 to 48.
Equipment	Hockey sticks, balls, pinnies to distinguish teams.
Area	Playing field (60 by 100 yards) marked as in illustration.
Skills	Dribbling, driving, bullying, fielding, dodging, positioning rules of field hockey.
Game	The object of the game is to hit the ball over the opponent's goal line. Players are divided into two teams, and members of each team are numbered. Team A forwards 1, 2, and 3 stand behind the center line. Team A halfbacks 4, 5, and 6 stand behind their forwards; the remaining players enter the zone area of their team and become goalkeepers. Team B players take corresponding positions at their end of the field.

The game is started by a bully on the center line by one player from each team. (The same procedure is followed after each goal and half time.) To bully the ball both players stand squarely facing the sidelines. Each player strikes alternately three times first the ground on his own side of the ball and then his opponent's stick. This completes the bully. The flat side of the stick only may be used for mak-

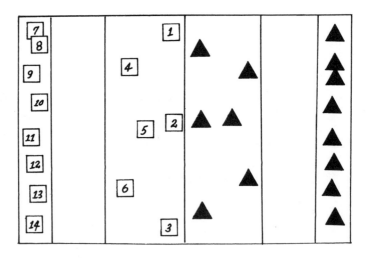

60 X 100 YARDS

ing contact with an opponent's stick at a bully. Every other player should be nearer his own goal than the ball, and should not stand within 5 yards of the ball until the bully is completed. No bully should be taken nearer than 5 yards from the end zone or 5 yards from the sideline.

When the bully is completed, the forwards may advance to the goal line of their opponents in an effort to hit the ball over the goal line. Halfbacks should never get ahead of their forwards. Their duty is to follow up their forwards so as to feed the ball to them if the forwards lose it. They, like the forwards, play their own positions. Forwards, while in their own half of the field near their own goal zone, should not drop behind the 25-yard line. The halfbacks should be there.

The goalkeepers of each team remain in their own zone areas and may not advance beyond the zone lines. They attempt to prevent the ball from crossing the goal line. They may use the stick to stop the ball that is on the ground. They are permitted to catch a lofted ball, if it is dropped immediately to the ground.

If the ball is hit with any part of the body or with the rounded side of the stick, or if the stick is raised above the shoulder, a free hit is awarded the opponents on the spot where the foul occurred. No player other than the striker should be within 5 yards of the spot where the free hit is made, and after taking the hit the striker should not play the ball until it has been touched or hit by another player. When the ball is hit over the sideline, off the stick of a player, a roll-in is taken by an opposing player. If the ball passes over the sideline off the stick of two opposing players, a bully is taken 5 yards on the field from the sideline.

Following a goal, players within each team rotate. Forwards go to the position of the highest numbered goalkeepers; halfbacks become forwards; goalkeepers become halfbacks.

The game is played in two halves of 15 minutes each. The time periods may be increased to 25-minute halves for older players. The teams exchange ends at half time.

Scoring   One point is scored each time the ball crosses the goal line. The team with the higher number of points at the end of the game wins.

Variations   None.

DODGING AND TACKLING

Players   Unlimited.

Equipment   Hockey sticks, balls, and pinnies.

Area   Playing field.

Skills   Stick-side, non stick-side, and scoop dodging; straight and left-hand lunge tackling, fielding, and driving.

Game   The object of the game is to hit the ball to the opposing line after attempting a dodge or tackle. Players are divided into two teams facing each other at a distance of 25 yards. The first player on team A drives the ball straight ahead toward team B and then follows the ball. The first player on team B runs to field the ball, controls it, and attempts to dodge the on-coming player from team A. If the dodge is successful, the dodger hits the ball to the second player on team A. Players move to the end of the opposite line. Each player has an opportunity to try a dodge and a tackle. The player that is successful in getting the ball to the opposite line scores 1 point. Repeat the pattern for at least two rounds.

Scoring   The team with the greatest number of points at the end of the second round is the winner.

Variations   (1) Stick-side, non stick-side, or scoop dodge may be used. (2) The opposing player may continue to tackle-back for a given distance.

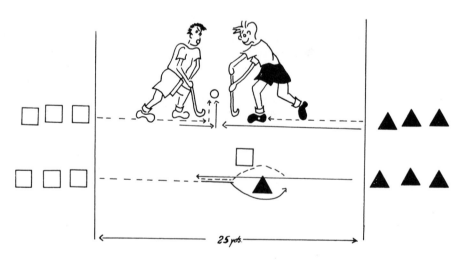

25 yds.

Players	Unlimited.
Equipment	Hockey sticks, balls, and objects.
Area	Regulation hockey field.
Skills	Scooping, dribbling, driving, and footwork.
Game	The object of the game is to execute three scoop strokes and hit the ball into the goal cage. Divide the players into equal teams. Teams each form a single column on the center line facing a goal cage. Balls are given to the first three players in each line. On a signal the first player scoops or lifts the ball over the center line with the stick, dribbles the ball to the 25-yard line, scoops the ball over the line, dribbles the ball to the striking circle, scoops the ball over the line, and drives for a goal. The player retrieves the ball and rolls to the fourth player in his line, thus keeping the line supplied with balls. Each player takes his turn and returns to the end of the line.
Scoring	Since the emphasis is on the scoop, each successful scoop is awarded 2 points. One point is awarded each time the ball enters the goal cage. The team with the greatest number of points is the winner.
Variations	Objects of various heights may be placed on the lines to make scooping more difficult.

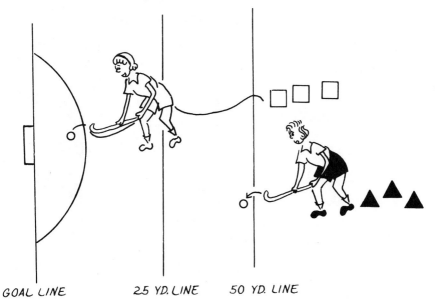

GOAL LINE   25 YD. LINE   50 YD. LINE

BULLY

Players   Unlimited.

Equipment   Hockey sticks and balls.

Area   Playing field.

Skills   Bullying, dribbling, and driving.

Game   The object of the game is for players to gain possession of the ball on the bully and then dribble and drive the ball to their own teams. The players are divided into two groups or teams, spaced facing each other 15 yards apart. Each player is given a number. The leader calls a number, and those players move to the center of the groups, bully, dribble, and drive the ball to their own team.

Scoring   Each time a player is successful in driving the ball to her team 1 point is scored.

Variations   Two or more numbers may be called at the same time. One player will execute the bully. The two players pass to each other to send the ball to their own team.

15 YDS.

GOALS

Players	Unlimited.
Equipment	Hockey sticks and balls.
Area	Playing field or gymnasium.
Skills	Dribbling, driving, passing, fielding, dodging, and tackling.
Game	The object of the game is to drive the ball below waist height over the opponent's goal line. The game is started with a bully by the centers, who attempt to get possession of the ball and pass to their own forward line. Only the forwards may drive the ball through the opponent's line. If a backfield player stops the ball, she passes to her forward line. When the ball goes out of bounds over the sideline, it is put into play with a roll-in. A free hit is awarded opponents for any fouls.
Scoring	One point is scored for each ball sent legally over the opponent's goal line. No point is scored if forward steps over the line while driving the ball. Game is restarted by center bully.
Variations	None.

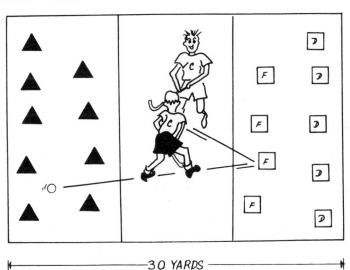

30 YARDS

Players	8 to 10 on a team. Unlimited.
Equipment	Hockey sticks, ball, pinnies, and benches.
Area	Playing field.
Skills	Dribbling, driving for accuracy, fielding, controlling ball, and footwork.
Game	The object of the game is to drive the ball under the bench. Divide the players into equal teams, with half of each team facing the other half 50 yards apart. The facing lines are not directly opposite. A bench is placed on the diagonal between the lines. The player dribbles straight ahead and executes a drive in an attempt to hit the ball under the bench toward the other half of her team. Players run to the end of the opposite line. When all players return to their original positions, the game is completed.
Scoring	Two points are awarded for each ball passing under the bench. The team with the highest score is the winner.
Variations	The left drive and left and right push passes may be used in place of the right drive.

Players	Unlimited.
Equipment	Hockey sticks, balls, goalkeeping equipment (goal pads, kickers, shoes), and goal cage.
Area	Regulation hockey field. Only the area in front of the goal cage is used.
Skills	Push passing or flicking at goal and goalkeeping skills.
Game	The object of the game is twofold: (1) for the offensive players to push the ball into the goal cage; and (2) for the goalkeeper to prevent the ball from entering the goal cage. This is an excellent game to improve the reaction time of a goalkeeper. The players are divided into equal teams and positioned in a semicircle 5 yards from the goal cage. The lines are numbered consecutively, and the leader varies the order when calling numbers. As the leader calls the number, the appropriate player attempts to push the ball into the goal cage. The leader should pause slightly after each number to give the goalkeeper an opportunity to move to the opposite side for the next shot. At the end of each round a new team moves forward to play the game.
Scoring	One point is scored for each ball that enters the goal cage. The team with the greatest number of points at the end of the playing period is the winner. The goalkeeper is not connected with any team.
Variations	None.

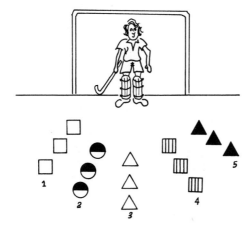

ALLEY BALL

Players	Unlimited.
Equipment	Hockey balls, hockey sticks, and targets.
Area	Playing field.
Skills	Rolling-in with left and right hands.
Game	The object of the game is to roll the ball as close to one side of the line as possible and hit the target. The group is divided into equal teams which each stand alongside a line. The players' sticks and feet must be on the side of the line opposite the side on which they roll the ball. Each player should have an opportunity to roll the ball with each hand.
Scoring	One point is scored each time the ball is legally rolled and hits the target.
Variations	Roll to player who dribbles across end line: first one across end line scores 1 point.

Players	Unlimited.
Equipment	Hockey sticks and balls.
Area	Hockey field.
Skills	Receiving passes from the rear, driving, dribbling, goal shooting, and goalkeeping.
Game	The object of the game is to hit the ball into the goal cage. Teams line up behind the center line with one forward near the 25-yard line. The halfback passes the ball to the forward, who dribbles and drives the ball into the goal cage or attempts to dodge the goalkeeper. The game begins with team 1 and progresses to team 5. The halfback then moves up to the forward position, while the forward moves to the end of the halfback line. The game continues until each player has an opportunity to shoot for a goal.
Scoring	One point is scored each time the ball crosses the goal line.
Variations	(1) The goalkeeper may have a fullback to play opposite each team. (2) One point is scored for the defensive team each time they gain possession of the ball.

TWO-MAN FIGURE EIGHT

Players	Unlimited.
Equipment	Hockey sticks and balls.
Area	Playing field or gymnasium.
Skills	Fielding, stick-side dodging, and push passing to the right.
Game	The object of the game is to improve the individual's footwork, stick-side dodge, and pass to the right. This is an excellent conditioning game. With players in couples, the ball is started by the player on the left who executes a push pass to the player on the right. The player on the right has moved to meet the ball, takes it into a stick-side dodge, and pushes the ball to the first player who is now on the right (see illustration). The team that reaches a given point first is the winner.
Scoring	Five points for first place, 3 points for second place, and 1 point for third place.
Variations	None.

Players Unlimited number of teams. One team has 6 defense players: goalkeeper, right fullback, left fullback, right halfback, center halfback, left halfback. The opponents have
8 attack players: left wing, left inner, center forward, right
inner, right wing, right halfback, center halfback, left halfback.

Equipment Hockey sticks, balls, and pinnies.

Area Regulation hockey field. One game played in each half of
the field, if sufficient coaches are available.

Skills Offensive tactics, defensive tactics, passing, fielding, driving, push passing, dodging, tackling.

Game The object of the game is: (1) to encourage the attacking
halfbacks to keep the ball in the scoring area; (2) to teach
the forwards to position themselves to receive passes from
their own halfbacks; and (3) to teach defensive players to
mark in the defensive striking circle.

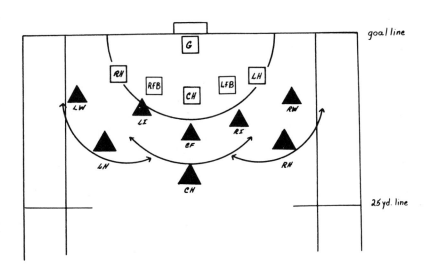

The game is started with the leader rolling the ball to one of the attacking halfbacks, who has taken a position outside the attacking striking circle, behind the forwards. The forwards create a space to receive a pass from the halfback by pulling away from the position of the ball. The forward, upon receiving the ball, drives for the goal, with the remaining forwards rushing the goalkeeper. If the goalkeeper clears the ball out of the striking circle, the forwards immediately move back into position to receive the ball again from a halfback.

Scoring One point is scored for the attacking team each time the ball is put into the goal cage. A point is scored for the defensive team each time the ball is hit over the 25-yard line. When a total of 5 points is scored by either team, new players are placed on the field by both teams.

Variations None.

Players   Unlimited number of teams. One team has 6 defense players: goalkeeper, right fullback, left fullback, right halfback, center halfback, left halfback. The opponents have 8 attack players: right wing, right inner, center forward, left inner, left wing, right halfback, center halfback, and left halfback.

Equipment   Hockey sticks and hockey balls.

Area   Regulation hockey field. One game played in each half of the field.

Skills   Driving, fielding, passing, push passing, dodging, tackling, marking.

Game   The object of the game is twofold: (1) for the offense to hit the ball into the goal cage; (2) for defense to hit the ball outside of the striking circle.

    The six defensive players, wearing pinnies, line up with feet and sticks behind the end line. They may not cross the line until the corner hit is taken. The five forwards line up with their feet and sticks outside the striking circle until the ball is hit. The three attacking halfbacks take positions behind the forwards, in case a forward should miss the ball.

The wing taking the corner hit drives to either inner, to the center forward, or to the center halfback and immediately moves to an onside position. The ball must travel fast, smoothly, and accurately to the receiver's stick side. (A weak hit will be intercepted by the outcoming defense.) The forwards wait until the ball is fielded by one player, who then drives the ball toward the goal, while the remaining forwards rush the goalkeeper. As soon as the wing takes the corner hit, the defensive players immediately move over the goal line and mark their respective opponents.

Ten corner hits are taken on alternate sides of the field. The attack attempts to put the ball into the goal cage, while the defense attempts to clear the ball out of the striking circle. New teams are placed on the field after ten corner hits have been taken.

Scoring The attacking team scores 1 point for each goal scored. The defensive team scores 1 point each time the ball is hit outside the striking circle. The team with the greatest number of points scored at the end of the playing time is the winner. A 3-minute time limit is set for each group if a point is not scored by either team.

Variations None.

COVERING

Players   Unlimited. Teams are divided into forwards, fullbacks, and goalkeepers. The forwards take the positions of left wing, left inner, right inner, and right wing, at the center line.

Equipment   Hockey sticks, balls, and pinnies.

Area   Regulation hockey field.

Skills   This game helps to teach fullbacks and goalkeepers the advanced skill of covering for each other. The forwards are practicing offensive strategy.

Game   The object of the game is twofold: (1) the attack must reach the striking circle or hit the ball into the goal cage; (2) the fullbacks must intercept the ball.

Each round is started by alternating the ball from left and right sides of the field. Usually, but not necessarily, the ball is started by the wing. If the ball is started on the left side of the field, the right fullback is up at the center line, marking the left inner. The left fullback is at the center of the field, near the striking circle, in a covering position. When the ball is put into play, the four forwards advance toward their goal. The opposing fullbacks attempt

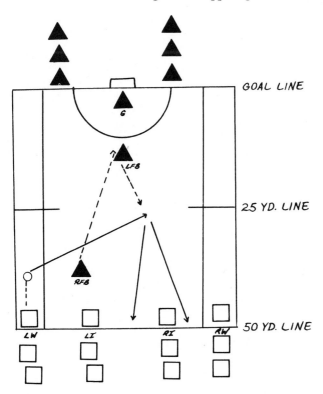

GOAL LINE

G

LFB

25 YD. LINE

RFB

50 YD. LINE

LW   LI   RI   RW

to intercept passes in order to prevent the forwards from reaching their goal. In the event that the forwards attempt a pass to the opposite side of the field, the covering back should anticipate the pass and move in to intercept it. If both fullbacks are passed by, the goalkeeper should be in a covering position to intercept the ball before a shot for goal.

Scoring Each time the forwards reach the striking circle 1 point is scored. Each time the fullback intercepts a pass 1 point is scored. If a goal is scored, 2 points are awarded.

Variations None.

LANE HOCKEY

Players Unlimited number of teams. 5 forwards and 5 defensive players.

Equipment Hockey sticks, balls, and pinnies.

Area Regulation hockey field. (50 by 100 yards)

Skills Dribbling, driving, dodging, tackling, fielding, passing, marking an opponent, and position play.

Game The object of the game is for the forwards or offensive team to hit the ball over the end line and for the defensive team to attempt to hit the ball over the center line. The five forwards take up their respective positions on the center line. The defensive team assumes position against the forwards. All players, with the exception of the fullbacks, must remain in their respective lanes. The fullbacks may play in any lane. A free hit is awarded to the opposing team when a player fails to remain in proper lane. The game may be started by any player on the forward line.

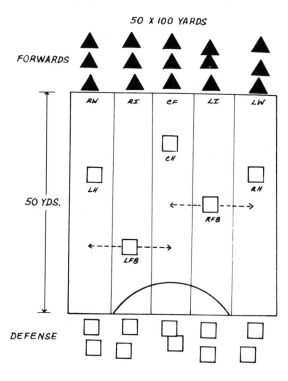

Scoring   One point is scored when the offensive team hits the ball over the end line. One point is scored for the defensive team when the ball is hit over the center line. After each goal is scored, new players substitute on each team. The team scoring the greater number of points is the winner.

Variations   None.

Lead-up Games Adaptable to Field Hockey

The following games, found elsewhere in this book, are considered to be suitable lead-up games for field hockey.

Base on Balls	124	Overtake Throw	114
Circle Line Soccer	95	Sideline Basketball	26
Circle Soccer	90	Target Pitch	119
End Ball	13	Wall Rebound (for goalkeepers)	63
Field Ball	21	Zig-Zag Throw	117
Keep Away	19		

LACROSSE

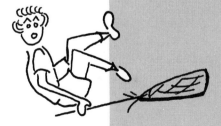

Lead-up Games Designed to Develop Lacrosse Skills

Lead-up games	Footwork	Cradling	Throwing	Catching	Picking-up	Pivoting	Cutting	Shooting	Intercepting	Dodging	Crosse checking	Drawing
On the whistle	X											
Twist	X	X										
Wall rebound		X	X	X								
Scat					X	X						
Long pass		X	X	X		X						
Throw ball			X	X								
Success			X	X								
Throw around		X	X	X								
Count off			X	X								
Circle pass		X	X	X								
Star lacrosse		X	X	X			X	X				
Half-field lacrosse		X	X	X	X	X	X	X	X	X		
Possession		X	X	X	X	X	X		X	X		
Pick-up					X	X					X	
Catch, go, and throw		X	X	X		X						
Draw		X	X	X	X	X	X		X	X		X
Interception			X						X			
Attack	X	X	X	X	X	X	X	X				
Rotation lacrosse	X	X	X	X	X	X	X	X	X	X	X	

Players Unlimited.

Equipment Lacrosse sticks and balls.

Area Playing field or gymnasium.

Skills Footwork (which is basic for all team sports), cradling, reverse turning, pivot turning.

Game The object of this game is to improve speed, quick change of direction, mobility of body, and general quality and ease of movement. The players may stand informally on the field or in lines. Each player has a ball in his crosse. On command of a whistle players run forward, backward, sideways to left, and sideways to right, changing direction frequently. Players cradle while running. On one whistle have players change direction with the pivot turn and good body twist. On two whistles have them change direction without the pivot turn.

Scoring No scoring.

Variations None.

TWIST

Players	8 on a team. Unlimited.
Equipment	Lacrosse sticks and balls.
Area	Playing field or gymnasium.
Skills	Cradling and preparation for dodging.
Game	The object of the game is to keep the ball in the crosse while cradling around the circle twisting away from each opponent. Two teams form a double circle facing opponents (as for grand right and left). Each player passes his opponent by right shoulder, next person by left, and so on, until each player reaches his original opponent again. Twisting the body away from the on-coming person and keeping head and crosse high, as in dodging, are emphasized. The game should be started by walking, then progress to running slowly, and finally progress to running rapidly.
Scoring	One point is awarded for each ball that remains in the crosse at the end of the third round. If several circles are competing, a single elimination tournament may be played.
Variations	None.

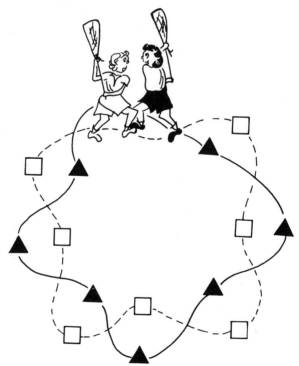

WALL REBOUND

Players   Unlimited.

Equipment   Lacrosse sticks and balls.

Area   Playing field or gymnasium with smooth wall.

Skills   Throwing and catching.

Game   The object of the game is to learn to throw and catch with the crosse. One player stands behind a line 15 feet from the wall. This player attempts to throw the ball against the wall as many times as he can without letting it fall to the ground. Other players should stand well behind him. His score is the number of successive passes that he makes. When the ball touches the floor, the next player on the team takes a turn.

Scoring   The team with the highest total score is the winner.

Variations   Players cradle the ball to a given line and throw the ball so that it bounces before hitting the wall. The ball is then caught in the crosse; player pivots and throws to the next player in his line.

SCAT

Players	10 to 50.
Equipment	Lacrosse sticks and balls.
Area	Playing field or gymnasium.
Skills	Picking up ground balls, pivoting, cradling.
Game	Players are divided into two lines facing each other about 20 feet apart. Players count off starting at opposite ends. The leader calls a number and says, "Attention," at which both persons of that number take one pace forward and execute right about face. When the leader calls, "Scat," both players pick up a ball from the ground with the crosse, and run around their line and back to their places, cradling.
Scoring	The first person back scores 1 point. Another number is called, and so on, until one team has scored 15 points.
Variations	None.

Players	Unlimited.
Equipment	Lacrosse sticks and balls.
Area	Playing field or gymnasium.
Skills	Cradling, pivoting, long passing, and catching.
Game	The object of the game is to learn to cradle, pivot, throw, and catch with accuracy. Number 1 cradles while running to a given line, pivots left or right, and throws the ball back to the next player in line. If the ball falls from the crosse, the player must retrieve it and continue from that spot.
Scoring	The team that returns first to its original position is the winner.
Variations	Various types of passes may be used.

25 YDS.

Players	Unlimited. Each team has 1 catcher.
Equipment	Lacrosse sticks, lacrosse ball or tennis ball, and two bases. Large circles may be marked on the playing area for first base and home base.
Area	Playing field or gymnasium.
Skills	Throwing and catching in the air and on the ground with the crosse.
Game	The object of the game is to throw the ball out into the field, run to first base, and return to home base before the fielders can return the ball to the catcher. Each player on the throwing team has an opportunity to throw the ball out into the field. If the runner can return to home base before the catcher touches home base with the ball in the crosse, a run is scored. The number of outs is unlimited. When each player has had an opportunity to throw the ball, the throwers exchange places with the fielders.
Scoring	The team with the greatest number of points after an even number of innings wins the game.
Variations	The runner may be required to cradle a ball in the crosse while running.

SUCCESS

Players   8 to 10 in a group.

Equipment   Lacrosse sticks and balls.

Area   Playing field or gymnasium.

Skills   Throwing and catching with a lacrosse stick.

Game   The object of the game is to become skilled in catching
the ball in the air or from a bounce with a lacrosse stick.
One player is the thrower while the others are fielders.
The thrower tosses high balls or grounders out into the
field. If a fielder can catch a fly ball or pick up a grounder
in the crosse, he becomes the thrower and the thrower becomes a fielder. If no fielder succeeds in catching or
stopping the ball, the first player to pick up the ball calls,
"Success." The thrower lays his stick on the ground parallel to the fielder, who tries to roll the ball over the stick.
If the ball hits or jumps over the stick, the fielder who
rolled the ball becomes the next thrower. If the ball misses
the stick, the same player continues to throw the ball to
the fielders.

Scoring   Each time a thrower continues to throw he scores 1 point.
The player with the greatest number of points at the end
of the playing period is the winner.

Variations   Various types of passes may be used.

FIELDERS' LINE

1ST BASE

HOME BASE

THROW AROUND

Players   16 to 36.

Equipment   Lacrosse sticks, balls, and four bases.

Area   Playing field, playground, or gymnasium. Area is marked off in a 35-foot square, or a softball diamond with 35-foot bases may be used.

Skills   Running, cradling, throwing and catching for accuracy with the lacrosse stick.

Game   The object of the game is for the team at home base to run the bases and return to home base before the fielding team can throw the ball around to each base. The players are divided into two teams. One team stands at home base. The members of the second team take their places in the field, with a player at each base and a catcher. On signal "Go" a team member at home base picks up a ball from the ground en route to first base and cradles as he runs the bases. At the same time the catcher throws the ball to the first baseman, that player throws it to the second baseman, the second baseman throws to the third baseman, and the latter throws the ball to the catcher. The ball must be thrown around the diamond during the time it takes the runner to return to home base. The ball must be thrown and caught with the crosse. However, the ball may be picked up in the crosse and thrown to the next base.

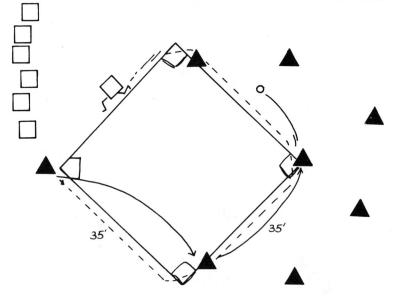

In the event that a baseman fails to catch the ball, an- other fielder may field the ball and throw to the proper base. After all members of a team have run, that team retires to the field.

Scoring If the baserunner reaches home base before the ball reaches the catcher, he scores 1 point for his team. If the fielding team returns the ball to the catcher before the baserunner reaches home base, the fielding team scores 1 point. The team that has the larger number of points after all players have run is the winner.

Variations Cradling when running the bases may be eliminated while the players are learning to throw and catch with the lacrosse stick.

COUNT OFF

Players 10 to 20 in a group.

Equipment Lacrosse sticks and balls. If a shortage of lacrosse sticks exists, use 2 sticks per group.

Area Playroom, playing field, or gymnasium.

Skills Throwing and catching.

Game The object of the game is to learn to throw and catch the ball successfully with the lacrosse stick. The players divide into equal teams, and each player is assigned a number. The leader places a ball in the crosse of one of the players of team A. The player with the ball calls out a number. The team B player with the called number steps out from his line, and the player from team A throws him the ball. If the player from B catches the ball in the crosse, he then calls out a team A number and throws him the ball. This pattern continues until the ball is missed, in which case the throwing team retains possession of the ball.

Scoring One point is scored for each successful catch. One point is lost for each wild throw. The team with the greatest number of points at the end of the playing period is the winner.

Variations Various types of passes may be used. Each player must run to receive the ball.

Players	6 to 8 on a team. Teams unlimited.
Equipment	Lacrosse sticks and balls.
Area	Playing field or gymnasium.
Skills	Catching, throwing, cradling, receiving left and right.
Game	Each team forms a circle with players facing clockwise. The players are numbered; number 1 takes a position inside the circle. The players who are forming the circle run clockwise. Each player raises his crosse to indicate where he would like to receive a pass from number 1. As each player catches the ball in the crosse and cradles the ball, he immediately throws the ball back to number 1. This play continues until number 1 has thrown the ball to each player in the circle. Number 2 then takes the center position, and game continues until each player on the team has been in the center.
Scoring	One point is awarded for each successful pass. The team with the greatest number of points at the end of the game is the winner.
Variations	Teams may change directions to practice receiving from the left and right.

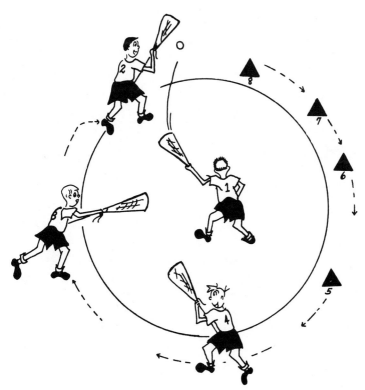

STAR LACROSSE

Players   5 to 40. The players are numbered off by 5's. Each group of 5 represents one team.

Equipment   Lacrosse sticks, balls, and goal cage.

Area   Playing field or gymnasium.

Skills   Catching on the run, running to meet the ball, indicating direction pass should take, leading a runner with a pass, overarm passing, underarm passing, shooting, and developing patterns for attack play.

Game   The five players assume a position on the field representing the five points of a star. The remaining teams line up behind them, that is, all of the number 1's in a line, the number 2's in another line, the number 3's, 4's, and 5's in separate lines. The five lines should then resemble a star, between the center of the field and the goal cage. Each player in line 1 should have a ball in his crosse. The number 1 player starts the game by throwing the ball to number 2, who passes the ball to number 3; number 3 passes to number 4, who passes to number 5. As number 5 catches the ball, number 1 is on his way toward the goal;

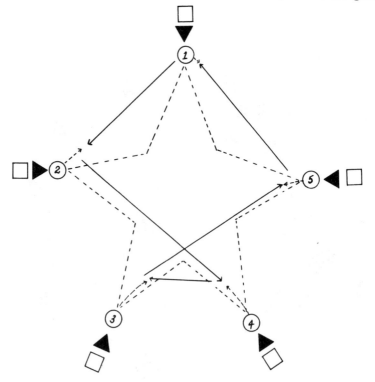

number 5 throws the ball to number 1, who shoots for a
goal. After each pass, the player runs to the end of that line to which he has thrown the ball. Number 1 moves to the end of line 2 after shooting for a goal. In this way, all five players are constantly moving to a new line until each player has an opportunity to shoot for goal. Each player runs forward to meet and catch the ball when the preceding player has the ball in his crosse. Each player should extend the crosse high above his head to indicate where he would like to receive the pass.

Scoring   One point is awarded for each successful catch. Two points are awarded for each ball that enters the goal cage. A score of 7 points would represent a perfect round. The team with the greatest number of points at the end of playing time is the winner. When all five positions have been played a perfect score of 35 could have been attained.

Variations   None.

HALF-FIELD LACROSSE

Players 12 to 24 players divided into regular lacrosse positions. If two full teams exist, one offense and defense plays half the field and the other plays the other half.

Equipment Lacrosse sticks, lacrosse balls, pinnies, and goal cages.

Area Regulation lacrosse field. Goal cages 90 to 110 yards apart.

Skills Throwing, catching, picking up from the ground or on a bounce, intercepting passes, marking, setting up attack or defensive plays.

Game The game is played with assigned positions, and at first each end of the field is a separate game. There will be a certain amount of delay in this game for the coach to show players correct spacing and to suggest various methods of attack. The defense players must be helped in techniques of marking and intercepting. When they have the ball they must be shown the desirability of immediately getting themselves and their sticks to the side of the field in order to make a pass up to their own attack. It is important that the two separate games be put together as one game before the end of the practice period, so that the feel of the relationship between defense and attack is not lost. Early in the season no checking of the stick should be allowed.

Scoring One point is scored when the attack scores a goal or the defense passes the ball to the center of the field and then to the leader.

Variations None.

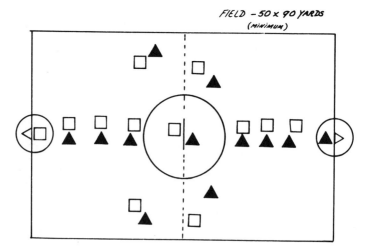

FIELD – 50 x 90 YARDS
(MINIMUM)

Players   10 to 30.

Equipment   Lacrosse sticks, lacrosse ball, tennis ball or hand ball, and pinnies.

Area   Playing field or gymnasium.

Skills   Stresses the importance of a defense player staying with an opponent. Throwing, catching, cradling, picking up ball, evading an opponent, and strategy.

Game   The object of the game is to pass and catch successfully. Players divide into equal teams, which may be differentiated by having players on one team wear pinnies. Two opposing players stand in the center of the playing area. The leader tosses the ball high into the air midway between the two players. The player who catches the ball attempts to pass it to another player on his team without his opponent's getting it. Players may not interfere with the throwing of the ball, but may intercept any pass. Any player may go after a ball in flight or a free ball, but he must not push or trip. The player with the ball in his crosse may not run with the ball more than 10 seconds. The leader makes the count aloud, and if the ball is not thrown within the 10-second period, the ball is awarded to the opposite team. For each foul a "free position" is awarded the opponents, and all players must be 10 yards away.

Scoring   Each successful pass scores 1 point. The team with the greatest number of points wins the game.

Variations   (1) This game may be played at a very early stage with the leader making all the passes and giving the ball to the player who has made the most correct cut, and with the players giving the ball back to the leader. One point is scored for each successful pass received. (2) Three consecutive caught passes counting as a goal would be another variation of the game.

PICK-UP

Players	20 to 40.
Equipment	Lacrosse sticks and balls.
Area	Playing field or gymnasium.
Skills	Picking up ground balls, pivoting, cradling, crosse checking.
Game	The object of the game is to pick up the ball and carry it across the goal line without losing it. Divide the group into two teams facing each other approximately 30 feet apart. The ball is placed midway between the two teams or goal lines. Players count off from opposite ends of the lines. The leader calls a number, and the players having that number race from their goal lines; each player tries to pick up the ball, pivot, and carry it across his goal line without the opponent's tapping the crosse lightly with his stick, causing the player to lose possession of the ball.
Scoring	Two points are awarded for crossing the goal line with the ball. One point for each legal crosse check that forces the ball from the opponent's crosse.
Variations	Call two or more numbers together.

CATCH, GO, AND THROW

Players   4 to 32.

Equipment   Lacrosse sticks and balls.

Area   Playing field or gymnasium.

Skills   Cradling, catching, pivoting, and passing.

Game   The object of the game is to make a successful catch, pivot, and pass. Squads are arranged in relay formation with lines 1, 2, 3, and 4 forming a square. The first player in line 1, with a ball in the crosse, runs toward the center of the square, does a rear pivot, and passes to the first player in line 2. The player in line 2 catches the ball, runs toward the center, pivots, and passes to line 3. The player in line 3 repeats the pattern, passing to line 4. Each player follows his own pass and moves to the end of the receiver's line.

Scoring   Each successful catch scores 1 point.

Variations   Various lacrosse techniques may be added.

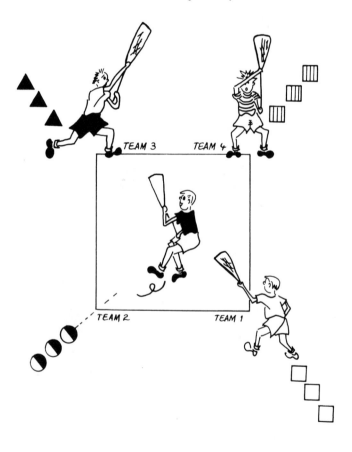

Players   6 to 30.

Equipment   Lacrosse sticks, ball, pinnies.

Area   Regulation lacrosse field or playing field. A center circle with a 10-yard radius is drawn in the center of the playing area.

Skills   Drawing, throwing, catching, picking up balls in the crosse, and guarding techniques.

Game   The object of the game is to make a successful draw or face-off and three successful passes. The players divide into equal teams, one of which wears pinnies. The teams' centers stand facing each other in the center of the circle, with their crosses back to back and parallel to the ground. The remaining players stand outside the center circle opposite an opponent. The leader places the ball between the two crosses. The ball is held in position by pressing the two sticks together. The signal "Draw" is given, and the centers press upward and to the side to release the ball. This is a free ball, and any player may catch it and pass to a teammate. When three successful passes have been made by either team, the ball is put into play again by a center draw.

Fouls: Body contact, any rough play, tapping an opponent's stick with the crosse.

Penalty: A free position is awarded to the opposing team with all other players 10 yards away.

Scoring For each three successive passes 1 point is awarded and the draw is repeated. The team with the greater number of points at the end of playing time is declared the winner.

Variations Goal lines may be drawn at each end of the field. When three successive passes have been made, the ball may be carried over the goal line to score 1 point.

Players	10 to 20 on a team. Teams unlimited.
Equipment	Lacrosse sticks and balls.
Area	Playing field or gymnasium.
Skills	Catching, evading an opponent, and pass interception.
Game	The object of the game is to make a successful catch while guarded by an opponent. The players are divided into equal teams. The two teams form straight lines, the interceptor's team on an angle and slightly ahead of the other line. The leader, standing approximately 20 feet away, tosses the ball midway between the first two players. One player attempts to catch the ball while the other attempts to intercept it.
Scoring	One point is scored for each successful catch.
Variations	The ball may be thrown directly toward one team while the other team attempts to intercept the pass. At the end of each round teams exchange places. Scoring: 1 point for each catch by the offensive team, 2 points for each interception by the defensive team.

ATTACK

Players	Unlimited. Players are divided into groups of 4.
Equipment	Lacrosse sticks, balls, and goal cage.
Area	Playing field.
Skills	Cradling, passing, catching, pivoting, goal shooting, creating spaces, and cutting to receive passes.
Game	The object of the game is to make a successful pass and shot for the goal. The game is intended to help the attack players become more conscious of being members of a team and of playing together. The purpose is to make the attacks pass quickly and space intelligently.

One member of each group of four is positioned at center, one at third home, one at second home, and one at first home (see illustration). Center passes the ball to third home, who runs on a diagonal to meet the ball; third home turns, runs, and passes to second home who has moved into the center of the field; second home turns, runs, and passes to first home. First home shoots for the goal. The ball moves in a straight line while the players go to meet it. The players rotate to each position.

Scoring	One point is scored for each pass that is caught. One point is scored for each ball that goes into the goal cage. The group of four with the highest number of points at the end of the playing period is the winner.
Variations	Various plays may be planned for varying the attack.

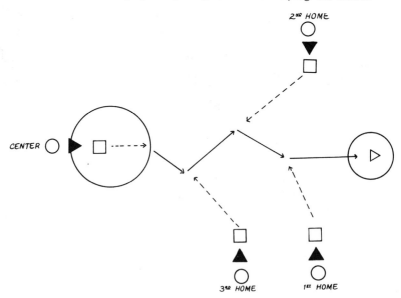

ROTATION LACROSSE

Players Unlimited.

Equipment Lacrosse sticks and tennis ball.

Area Regulation hockey field or soccer field.

Skills Cradling, passing, catching, dodging, pivoting, goal shooting, positioning, offensive and defensive strategy.

Game The object of the game is to throw the ball into the goal with the lacrosse stick. The teams line up as shown in the illustration at the start of the game and following each goal. Games are played in 5-minute quarters. Rotate teams at the beginning of each quarter.

    The leader rolls the ball on the ground between the two center forwards who attempt to gain possession by picking up the ball with the lacrosse stick. Players advance the ball by running, dodging, pivoting, or passing until one player is in position to attempt a shot at the goal. The try must be made while outside the restraining circle (or goalkeeper's area). Within this restricted area, where no other player is permitted, the goalkeeper may stop, catch, and throw the ball with the crosse. The goalkeeper is permitted to use the legs in stopping a ball. A player on defense may obtain possession of the ball by striking the offensive player's stick using an underhand tap to dislodge the ball. Players on both defense and offense must attempt to cover their own areas of the field in order to insure balanced team play and also to allow all players an opportunity to get into the action. Defense players may not

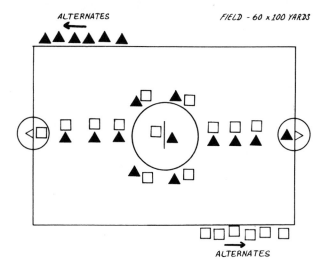

ALTERNATES

FIELD - 60 x 100 YARDS

ALTERNATES

cross the center line. Forwards may not retreat beyond the two-thirds of the field line. On a throw-in from out of bounds opponents must be at least 5 yards away.

FOULS: Tripping, pushing, holding an opponent's stick, hitting downward with the stick.

PENALTY: A free shot at the goal taken outside the restraining circle. The goalkeeper is permitted to remain at the goal cage to prevent the ball from entering the cage. When the ball crosses the sideline an opponent is awarded a throw-in.

Scoring   One point is scored for each goal. The team with the greater number of points at the end of each quarter is the winner.

Variations   The alternate teams may line up along the sideline. The ball may be passed to them, but they are not permitted to enter the playing field.

Lead-up Games Adaptable to Lacrosse

The following games, found elsewhere in this book, are considered to be suitable lead-up games for lacrosse.

SOCCER

SPEEDBALL

SPEED-A-WAY

Lead-up Games Designed to Develop
Soccer–Speedball*–Speed-A-Way Skills †

Basic skills involved

Lead-up games	Kicking	Trapping	Passing	Blocking	Dribbling	Heading	Goal keeping	Goal shooting	Tackling	Volleying	Conversion	Throwing	Catching
Norwegian ball	X												
Pin-ball soccer	X	X											
Soccer dodgeball	X	X	X										
Circle soccer	X	X	X	X									
Triangle soccer	X	X	X	X									
Mickey mouse					X								
Teacher ball	X	X	X			X			X				
Net soccer						X			X				
Circle line soccer	X	X	X				X	X					
Line kick	X	X	X	X	X								
Line soccer	X	X	X	X	X				X				
Long-base soccer	X	X	X				X	X	X				
Mass soccer	X	X	X	X	X	X			X	X			
Sideline soccer	X	X	X	X	X	X	X	X	X	X			
Three-zone soccer	X	X	X	X	X	X	X	X	X	X			
Rotation soccer	X	X	X	X	X	X	X	X	X	X			
Alley soccer	X	X	X	X	X	X	X	X	X	X			
Modified soccer	X	X	X	X	X	X	X	X	X	X			
Crab soccer	C	O	N	D	I	T	I	O	N	I	N	G	
Toe pick-up										X			
Two-legged lift											X	X	X
Circle conversion											X	X	X

---

* Speedball is a game originated by Elmer D. Mitchell. In speedball the ball may be played with the hands when it goes directly into the air from a player's foot. This is a conversion of a ground ball to an aerial ball and is the essential difference between speedball and soccer. These lead-up games have been designed to develop these conversion skills.

† Speed-a-way is a game originated by Marjorie S. Larsen. It combines the skills of soccer (kicking, dribbling, heading), speedball (throwing and catching an aerial ball), and touch football (running with an aerial ball and tagging). For a fuller description of the game, sources are listed in the selected references at the end of the book.

A game similar to speed-a-way, called gator ball, is widely played in Florida.

Players 8 to 10 on a team. Teams unlimited.

Equipment Soccer balls.

Area Playground or gymnasium.

Skills Kicking.

Game The object is for the kicker to kick the ball and to run around his team a predetermined number of times before the team in the field can form a line in straddle position and roll the ball through everyone's legs to the end person, who holds the ball in the air. The ball can be kicked in any direction in front of the kicker. The fielders are scattered until the ball is kicked. They then line up behind the person who recovers the ball. The ball must pass through everyone's legs except those of the last person, who holds the ball in the air over his head. If the fielding team performs this feat before the runner can circle his team, three times generally, the kicker fails to score. After everyone has kicked, teams change sides.

Scoring One point is scored by the kicker if he can circle his team three times before the last person in line raises the ball.

Variations Have the kicker dribble a second ball once around his team instead of running three times.

PIN-BALL SOCCER

Players   8 to 10 on a team. Teams unlimited.

Equipment   Soccer balls and Indian clubs or milk cartons.

Area   Playground or gymnasium.

Skills   Kicking and trapping.

Game   The object is to knock down the Indian clubs. Indian clubs
              are placed midway between the two teams. The teams on
              alternate kicks try to knock down the clubs. The kicks
              must be taken from behind the lines.

Scoring   The team knocking down the most Indian clubs is the
              winner.

Variations None.

SOCCER DODGEBALL

Players   8 to 10 on a team. Teams unlimited.

Equipment   Soccer balls.

Area   Playground or gymnasium. (30-foot circle)

Skills   Kicking, trapping, and passing.

Game   The object is for the players who form a circle to hit the players inside the circle below the shoulders with the ball. The ball is kicked by the outside players, and the inside players may not use their hands. Players in the center are not eliminated. After a predetermined time the teams change places.

Scoring   One point is scored for the kicking team each time a person in the center is hit. The team scoring the most hits is the winner.

Variations   (1) Use several balls. (2) Center team forms small circle. Outer team tries to kick the ball between the players in inner circle. The team that succeeds in the shortest time is the winner.

CIRCLE SOCCER

Players   8 to 10 on a team. Teams unlimited.

Equipment   Soccer balls.

Area   Playground or gymnasium. (30-foot circle)

Skills   Kicking, trapping, blocking, and passing.

Game   Each team forms a semicircle; two opposing teams, or two semicircles, then join to form one circle. The object is to kick the ball below shoulder level between members of the other team. After each score, the players rotate one place to the right. If a ball comes to rest inside the circle, a player from that half of the circle may get the ball and take it to the circle and start again.

Scoring   One point is scored each time the ball goes through the opponent's team below the shoulder level. One point is also scored against a team that uses hands to stop the ball.

Variations   (1) Play in a line or square formation. (2) Players hold hands.

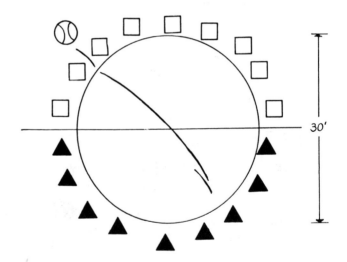

30'

Players	10 on a team. Teams unlimited.
Equipment	Soccer ball.
Area	Playground or gymnasium. (35-foot square)
Skills	Kicking, trapping, blocking, and passing.
Game	Players form a square, with each team representing two adjacent sides of the square. The object is for two "active" players to kick the ball below shoulder level through the other team. After each score two new players become active. The active players play in their own triangle, or half court, while the others serve as line guards. Line players may block the ball with their bodies but cannot use their hands. After each score the team scored against puts the ball in play.
Scoring	One point is scored each time the ball goes below shoulder level through the opponent's team.
Variations	Use more than two active players.

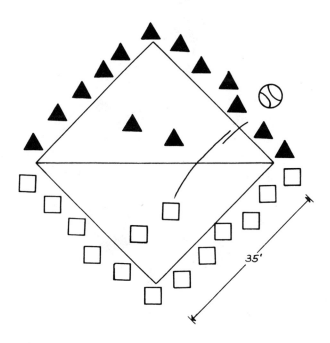

MICKEY MOUSE

Players	8 to 10 on a team. Teams unlimited.
Equipment	Soccer balls.
Area	Playground or gymnasium. (30-foot circle)
Skills	Dribbling.
Game	The object is for a player, when his number is called, to run to the center of the circle and dribble the ball as fast as he can out through his opening, around the circle, and in through the same opening to the center of the circle, where he finishes by placing his foot on the ball. Players should stay seated until their number is called to maintain uniform circles.
Scoring	The person finishing first scores 1 point for his team. Team with the most points is declared the winner.
Variations	Have the dribbler weave in and out of the players as he goes around the circle.

|←————30′————→|

Players   8 to 10 on a team. Teams unlimited.

Equipment   Soccer balls.

Area   Playground or gymnasium.

Skills   Heading, volleying, passing, and trapping.

Game   The object is for each team to perform the designated skill
               in the quickest possible time. Each team member, in turn,
               serves as leader for each skill by taking the center position.
               He then performs the skill with each team member, one
               by one. When he is finished, a new leader takes over.

Scoring   One point is scored for each team successfully completing
               the skill in the shortest time.

Variations   (1) Perform only one skill. Do it several times around.
               (2) See which team can head or volley the ball the long-
               est without allowing the ball to hit the ground.

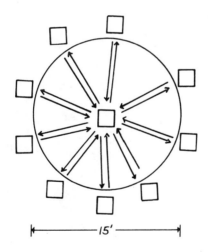

NET SOCCER

Players   8 to 10 on a team. Teams unlimited.

Equipment   Soccer ball, volleyball net, and standards.

Area   Playground or gymnasium. (25 by 50 feet)

Skills   Heading and volleying.

Game   The object is to head or volley the ball back and forth over the net until the opponent lets the ball hit the ground or knocks it out of bounds. The ball may be headed or volleyed on one side of the net as many times as is necessary to return it to the other team. The server puts the ball in play with a punt that must go directly over the net. Volleyball rules are in effect for scoring and rotation.

Scoring   One point is scored by the serving team each time the other team fails to return the ball properly.

Variations   (1) Allow the ball to bounce once. (2) Use a volleyball or beachball with beginners.

25' X 50'

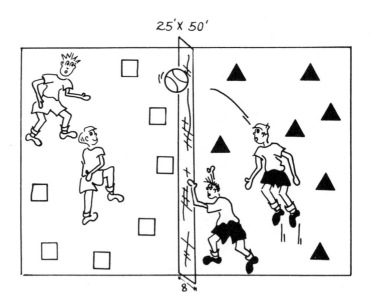

8'

Players   8 to 10 on a team. Teams unlimited.

Equipment   Soccer ball.

Area   Playground or gymnasium.

Skills   Kicking, trapping, blocking, passing, and goalkeeping.

Game   The object is for each team to kick the ball, below shoulder level, over the goal line, which is the diameter of the inner circle. Each team has a goalkeeper, three forwards, and several fielders. Each goalkeeper plays inside the inner circle on the opposite side of the center line from his team. The forwards play between the two circles, and the fielders outside the circle. Only the goalie may use his hands. Either forwards or fielders may score. When a goalie stops a ball, he passes it to his fielders. After each score players rotate positions.

Scoring   One point is scored each time a forward or fielder kicks the ball below shoulder level across the goal line.

Variations   Use more than one ball.

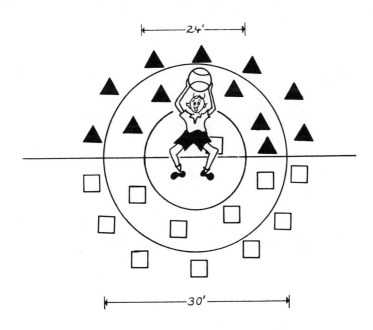

LINE KICK

Players 8 to 10 on a team. Teams unlimited.

Equipment Soccer ball.

Area Playground or gymnasium. (30 feet between lines)

Skills Kicking, blocking, trapping, passing, and tackling.

Game The game starts with the ball on a spot midway between two facing teams. A number is called and the player from each team with this number runs forward and attempts to gain possession of the ball so he can return it to his team. This center player recovers the ball in the center and returns it to the linemen of his own team. The linemen attempt to kick the ball through the other team. Only the linemen can score in this game. After a score a new number is called.

Scoring One point is scored each time a lineman kicks the ball below the shoulders through the other line.

Variations (1) Play in a circle or square formation. (2) When a center player gains control of the ball, he tries to knock down an Indian club designated for his team.

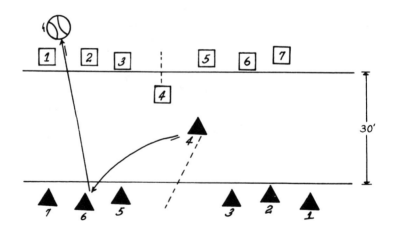

Players	8 to 10 on a team. Teams unlimited.
Equipment	Soccer ball.
Area	Playground or gymnasium. (30 feet between lines)
Skills	Dribbling, kicking, passing, tackling, trapping, and goal-keeping.
Game	The object is for the "active" players to score by kicking the ball below shoulder level through the other team. The line players act as goalies and are permitted to use their hands. As soon as the ball is caught by a lineman, it must be passed to an active player on his team. The game starts with the ball on a spot midway between the two lines, by a roll-in, or by a dropped ball. After a score, new numbers are called. Only the active players can score.
Scoring	One point is scored by an active player kicking the ball below shoulder level through the other team.
Variations	(1) Players form a square or circle formation. (2) Call more than one number at a time. (3) Have four teams, one lined up on each side of a square. When a number is called, the four persons with that number are against each other. Each player has the possibility of scoring on three sides of the square.

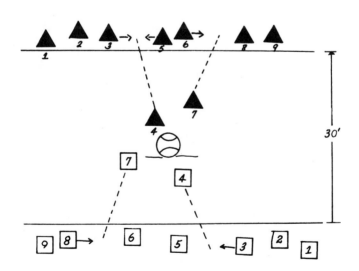

LONG-BASE SOCCER

Players	8 to 10 on a team. Teams unlimited.
Equipment	Soccer ball.
Area	Playground or gymnasium. (Base 50 feet away)
Skills	Kicking, trapping, passing, and goal shooting.
Game	When the game starts, one team is at bat at the goal line and one is in the field. The object is for those at bat to kick the ball, run around long base, and return home without being hit by the ball or having the ball cross the goal line ahead of them. Everyone on both teams has a number. The first person comes to bat while his corresponding number on the fielding team comes to the pitching position. The pitcher rolls the ball, and the batter attempts to kick the ball as far as possible. Any ball kicked in front of the goal line is considered a fair ball. After the ball is kicked, the batter runs around long base and back to the goal line. The members of the fielding team have two ways of putting him out. They can either hit him with a kicked ball or pass to his corresponding number in the field, who then kicks the ball behind the goal line. The

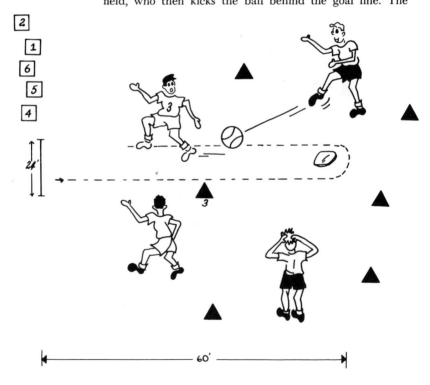

fielders may not use their hands. Teams change sides when all members on a team have batted. A batter is allowed to run out of the base line to avoid being hit.

Scoring One point is scored each time the batter can circle long base and cross the goal line ahead of the ball without being hit.

Variations (1) Omit the pitcher. Have the batter punt, drop kick, or place kick from the goal line. (2) Use two balls. After the batter kicks the ball, he dribbles a second ball around long base and back across the goal line. (3) As the fielding team becomes more proficient, use a goalkeeper. The batter on deck plays goalie, that is, batter number 3 bats, batter number 4 plays goalie.

MASS SOCCER

Players 10 on a team. Teams unlimited.

Equipment Soccer ball.

Area Playground or gymnasium. (30 by 60 yards)

Skills All the fundamental soccer skills.

Game The object is to kick the ball below shoulder level over the opponent's end line. Teams line up behind their end lines. The ball is placed in the center of the field. The players rush for the ball and attempt to kick it over the opposing end line. There are no assigned positions. When the ball goes over the sideline, it is thrown back in by the referee. No one is allowed to use his hands.

Scoring One point for every time the ball crosses the opponent's goal line below shoulder level.

Variations (1) Use two balls to provide more action. (2) Divide the team into three equal groups: goalies on the end line, sideline players along both sidelines in their half of the field, and forwards on the playing field. Rotate groups after each score.

30 X 60 YARDS

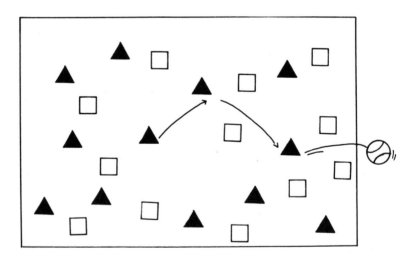

Players	20 on a team. Teams unlimited.
Equipment	Soccer ball.
Area	Playground or gymnasium. (30 by 60 yards)
Skills	All the fundamental skills of soccer.
Game	Each team is made up of ten active players and ten sideline players. The object is for the active players to kick the ball over the end line of the other team. None of the players may play the ball with his hands. The active players play regular soccer positions and rules. Following a score the active players are rotated with sideline players. Sideline players keep the ball from going out of bounds and pass it back to one of their active players. They can be used to advance the ball; however, goals must be made by active players. The active players on the end line serve as goalies. Play is started by the referee dropping the ball between two opposing players.
Scoring	One point is scored by an active player kicking the ball below shoulder level over the other team's end line.
Variations	Use a soccer goal and goalkeeper.

30 X 60 YARDS

THREE-ZONE SOCCER

Players   10 on a team. Teams unlimited.

Equipment   Soccer ball.

Area   Playground or gymnasium. (30 by 60 yards)

Skills   All the fundamental skills of soccer.

Game   Each team is divided into three equal groups of goalies, halfbacks, and forwards. The object is for the forwards to kick the ball, below shoulder level, over the end line past the goalies. The goalies are on the end lines, the halfbacks in the middle zone of the field, and the forwards between the halfbacks and the opposing goalies. The game is started by a dropped ball between two opposing halfbacks in the center of the field. The halfbacks try to get the ball to their forwards. All players must remain in their zone. Goalies may use their hands. Players rotate after each score.

Scoring   One point is scored each time the ball is kicked below shoulder level by a forward over an opponent's end line.

Variations   None.

30 X 60 YARDS

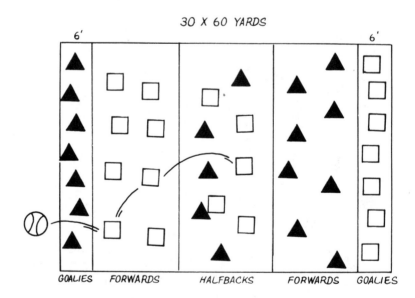

GOALIES   FORWARDS   HALFBACKS   FORWARDS   GOALIES

Players	9 or 12 on a team. Teams unlimited.
Equipment	Soccer ball.
Area	Playground or gymnasium. (30 by 60 yards)
Skills	All the fundamental skills of soccer.
Game	Each team, divided into three equal groups of forwards, guards, and goalies, lines up. The object is for the forwards to kick the ball below shoulder level over their opponent's end line. Whenever a point is scored, positions are rotated within each team. The forwards play in their opponent's half of the field except on the kickoff, the guards play in their own half of the field, and the goalies are on the end line. The goalies may use their hands to defend the goal. The game is started with a kickoff at the center, with every player in his own half of the field. After each score, the team scored against kicks off.
Scoring	One point is scored by a forward kicking the ball over the other team's end line below shoulder level.
Variations	None.

30 X 60 YARDS

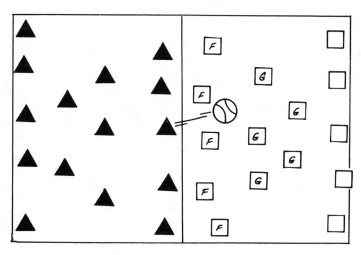

LINE UP FOR KICK OFF

ALLEY SOCCER

Players 10 on a team. Teams unlimited.

Equipment Soccer ball.

Area Playground or gymnasium. (30 by 60 yards)

Skills All the fundamental skills of soccer.

Game Each team has five alley players; other players are goalies. The object is for alley players, while remaining in their respective alleys, to kick the ball below shoulder level over the other team's end line. The game is started by a dropped ball at midfield between the two center alley players. Each player must remain in his own alley but may run the full length of his alley. The penalty for going out of the alley is loss of the ball. The opposing team gets a free kick at the spot of the penalty. After each score, alley players and goalies exchange positions.

Scoring One point is scored each time the ball crosses the end line below the shoulders of the goalies.

Variations (1) Use fewer alleys. (2) Use a goal and goalkeeper. (3) Have sideline players.

30 X 60 YARDS

Players	8 to 10 on a team. Teams unlimited.
Equipment	Soccer ball.
Area	Playground or gymnasium. (30 by 60 yards)
Skills	All the fundamental skills of soccer plus corner kicks, goal kicks, and penalty kicks.
Game	The object is to advance the ball across the other team's goal line. The game is like regular soccer without position play. Each team has a goalkeeper, and the rest of the players are either guards or forwards. The forwards generally play ahead of the guards as the ball is moved down the field. Soccer rules apply.
Scoring	One point is scored when the ball passes over the opponent's goal line.
Variations	(1) The forwards are restricted to the opponent's half of the field and the guards to their own half. (2) Place two Indian clubs in the goal area, and do not allow anyone in this area. One point is scored by knocking down a club. This variation does away with the goalkeeper; otherwise the game is the same.

30 X 60 YARDS

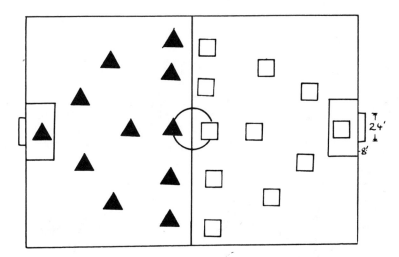

CRAB SOCCER

Players 15 on a team. Teams unlimited.

Equipment Soccer, cage, or medicine ball.

Area Gymnasium or playfield. (40 by 60 feet)

Skills Conditioning.

Game The object is to move the ball over the opponent's end line while maintaining the crab-walk position. The hands cannot be used to advance the ball. The game starts with each team lined up on its own end line and the ball in the middle of the playing area. On the signal both teams move toward the ball in the center and attempt to kick it over the opposing end line. The game is very similar to mass soccer except for the crab-walk position. The game is made more exciting by the use of a cage ball.

Scoring One point for every time the ball crosses the opponent's end line.

Variations (1) Use soccer goals. Score 5 points for a goal and 1 point for the passing of the ball over the end line. (2) Divide the team into guards and forwards. Let the forwards roam and have the guards protect the end line. Rotate after a score.

40' X 60'

24'

Players	8 to 10 on a team. Teams unlimited.
Equipment	Soccer balls.
Area	Playground or gymnasium.
Skills	Passing, trapping, and conversion.
Game	The object is to see which team can be first to convert successfully a ground ball to an aerial ball. Each team assumes shuttle formation. The first player in one line passes the ball with his feet to the first player in the opposite line. The receiving player traps the ball with the sole of his foot and then applies pressure downward and snaps the foot back at the same time. As the ball rolls toward him, he places the same foot used for the snapback under the ball and raises the ball to his hands. This player then rolls the ball to the second player in the other line. Each player runs to the end of the opposite line when his turn is completed. Play continues until each player is back in his original position.
Scoring	The team finishing first is the winner.
Variations	Use other forms of conversion.

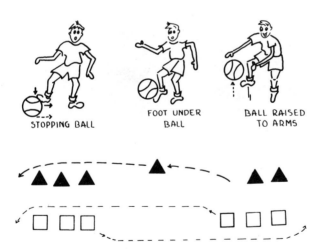

STOPPING BALL

FOOT UNDER
BALL

BALL RAISED
TO ARMS

TWO-LEGGED LIFT

Players	8 to 10 on a team. Teams unlimited.
Equipment	Soccer balls.
Area	Playground or gymnasium.
Skills	Conversion, throwing, and catching.
Game	The object is to see which team can be first to convert successfully a ground ball to an aerial ball. One player on each team, who acts as leader, stands facing the line of other players; he is about 10 feet in front of them. He rolls the ball slowly to the first player in the line, who traps the ball between his ankles or calves. He jumps with the knees flexed, releases the ball in an upward direction, and catches it before it hits the ground. He then throws the ball back to the leader. The leader rolls the ball to each player on the team. After everyone has served as leader, the game is over.
Scoring	The team finishing first is the winner.
Variations	Use other forms of conversion.

CIRCLE CONVERSION

Players	8 to 10 on a team. Teams unlimited.
Equipment	Soccer balls.
Area	Playground or gymnasium.
Skills	Conversion, throwing, and catching.
Game	The object is to see which team can be first to convert different types of ground balls into aerial balls. Players form a circle with one player in the center. The center player throws, bounces, or rolls the ball to each player in the circle. The players in the circle convert each ball into an aerial ball and pass it back to the player in the center. At the end of each round a new player takes the center. After each player has had an opportunity in the center, the game is finished. The following conversions may be used:

KNEE KICK: As a high bouncing ball is falling from its peak height, the player flexes one knee, which causes the ball to bounce upward off the knee, so that it may be caught.

LEG ROLL: As the ball rolls toward the player, the foot is extended so that the ball will roll up the leg permitting the player to catch it.

KNEE KICK

INSTEP LIFT

LEG ROLL

INSTEP KICK: As the ball rolls toward the player, he lifts it up with the instep of the foot and flexes the knee in a sideward and upward direction raising the ball to himself.

Scoring   The team finishing first is the winner.

Variations   Use other forms of conversion.

Lead-up Games Adaptable to Soccer, Speedball, and Speed-a-way

The following lead-up games, found elsewhere in this book, can easily be adapted to lead up to soccer, speedball, and speed-a-way, by substituting a soccer ball and the soccer skills one wishes to develop. All the basketball lead-up games involving throwing and catching can be used for speedball and speed-a-way.

Around the Clock	38	Hit and Stop	33
Base on Balls	124	Keep Away	19
Basketball Relay	15	Kick Ball	121
Boundary Ball	143	Kick Over	145
Bull in the Ring	10	Leader Ball	168
Circle Pass	71	Long Pass	65
Circle Target	11	Obstacle Dribble	37
Count Off	70	On the Whistle	61
Covering	55	Scat	64
Diagonal Shuttle	46	Shooting Goals	49
Dodging and Tackling	42	Star Lacrosse	72
Dribble Contest	14	Target Pitch	119
Drop-Kick Contest	146	Team Pepper	125
End Zone	144	Team Pin Guard	9
Flicks	47	Triangles	36
Guard Ball	8	Wall Rebound	63
Hit Away	34	Zig-Zag Throw	117

SOFTBALL

Lead-up Games Designed to Develop Softball Skills [*]

Lead-up games	Basic skills involved					
	Base running	Throwing	Catching	Fielding	Pitching	Batting
Around the bases	X					
Overtake throw		X	X			
Softball pop-up		X	X			
Bat ball		X	X	X		
Zig-zag throw		X	X		X	
Around the horn	X	X	X			
Target pitch					X	
Danish rounders	X	X	X	X		
Kick ball	X	X	X	X		
Throw softball	X	X	X	X		
Line ball			X	X		X
Base on balls	X	X	X	X		X
Team pepper			X		X	X
Cricket softball		X	X	X		X
Home-run derby			X	X		X
Circle softball			X	X	X	X
Long ball		X	X	X	X	X
Hit pin softball	X	X	X	X	X	X
One old cat	X	X	X	X	X	X

---

[*] It is suggested that a batting tee be used occasionally in the beginning lead-up games until the batting skills are developed to a point where the players are proficient enough to have some success in hitting a ball.

Players 6 on a team. Teams unlimited.

Equipment None.

Area Playground or gymnasium. (45-foot bases)

Skills Base running.

Game The object is for a team to be the first to have everyone run the bases. The teams line up on the inside of the diamond at diagonally opposite bases. The first person makes one complete circuit of the bases and then touches off the second player, who does the same thing.

Scoring The team finishing first is the winner.

Variations None.

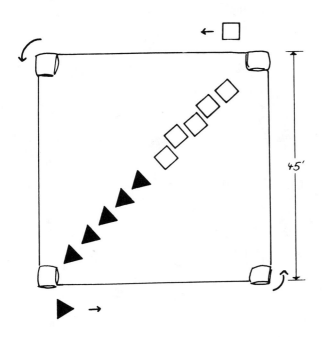

Players	6 to 8 on a team. Teams unlimited.
Equipment	Softballs.
Area	Playground or gymnasium. (30-foot circle)
Skills	Throwing and catching.
Game	The teams form one circle with players of opposing teams alternating. A captain of each team is in the center of the circle, and each has a ball. The captains start their balls on opposite sides of the circle; both balls are passed clockwise. On a signal the captain throws the ball to his players in turn and receives a return throw. The object is for one team to throw and catch the ball so rapidly that it overtakes the other team's ball. After each round a new captain goes into the center.
Scoring	The team that is able to overtake the other team is the winner.
Variations	(1) Enlarge the circle. (2) Use various kinds of throws, for example, toss, underhand pitch.

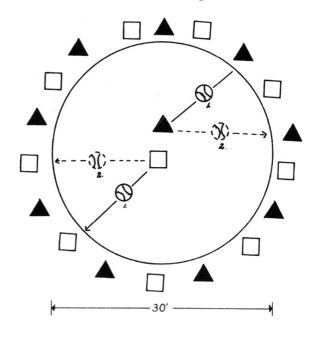

Players	6 to 8 on a team. Teams unlimited.
Equipment	Softball.
Area	Playground. (50-foot circle)
Skills	Throwing and catching high fly balls.
Game	The object is for the fielding team, scattered informally in the center of a large circle, to catch the fly balls thrown by the throwing team, who forms the circle. Each member of the throwing team, in turn, throws the ball as high into the air as possible. The player in the field who has a corresponding number attempts to catch the ball before it touches the ground in the prescribed area. When everyone has thrown, teams exchange roles.
Scoring	One point is scored by the throwing team each time the ball drops in the prescribed area without being caught.
Variations	Have the ball batted instead of thrown.

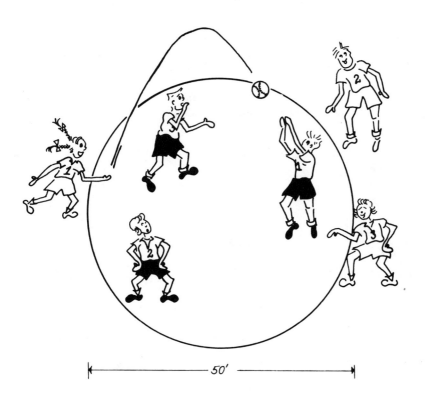

BAT BALL

Players   6 to 8 on a team. Teams unlimited.

Equipment   Playground ball or volleyball.

Area   Playground or gymnasium. (30 by 50 feet)

Skills   Throwing, catching, and fielding.

Game   The object is for the batter to hit the ball into fair territory, circle the far base, and return home without being hit by the ball. The batter bats the ball with his hand or fist so that it crosses the short line; he then attempts to run around the far base and back home without being hit. The members of the fielding team field the ball and attempt to hit the runner with it. The fielders may not walk with the ball or hold the ball longer than 3 seconds. The runner is not permitted to stop or to run out of the baseline. After everyone bats, sides change.

Scoring   One point is scored each time a player successfully runs around the far base to home plate without being hit.

Variations   (1) Use three outs to retire a side. (2) Give the fielders a choice of hitting the runner or throwing to their catcher at home plate ahead of the runner. (3) The fielders must make five passes involving five different players before they may hit the runner. (4) Have a mat between home and far base where the runner has to perform a stunt going and returning, for example, a forward roll.

Players	8 to 10 on a team. Teams unlimited.
Equipment	Softballs.
Area	Playground or gymnasium. (30 feet between lines)
Skills	Throwing, catching, and pitching.
Game	The object is for a team to throw or pitch the ball through the zig-zag pattern in the shortest time. Each team is divided evenly into two lines facing each other. The first person in one line throws the ball across to the first person in the other line, and so on down the line. When the person at the foot of the line receives the ball, he throws diagonally to the first person in the other line and then goes to the head of his own line. This continues until everyone is back in his original position.
Scoring	The team finishing first is the winner.
Variations	Use underhand pitching.

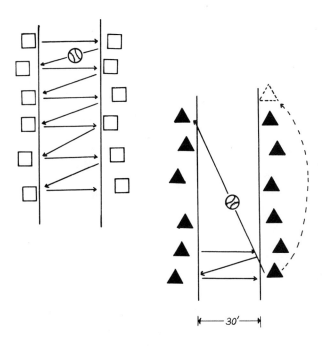

AROUND THE HORN

Players	8 on a team. Teams unlimited.
Equipment	Softball.
Area	Playground or gymnasium. (45-foot bases)
Skills	Throwing, catching, and base running.
Game	The object is for the fielders to relay the ball around the bases twice before the runner can run the bases once. Two fielders are stationed at each base. One fielder takes the first throw, and the other takes the throw the second time around. The game starts with the runner tagging home ready to run to first. His goal is to touch each base and tag home. The catcher has the ball at home and throws to first on the signal. The fielders must not interfere with the runner and should stand back from the base unless one of them is catching the ball. Each fielder must touch the base with his foot while he has the ball, before he can throw to the next base. After each runner has a turn, sides change.
Scoring	One point is scored for each successful run.
Variations	(1) Change the number of times around the bases for the runners and the throwers. (2) Adjust the distance between bases to the ability of the players. (3) Have the batter bunt the ball while the basemen field the bunt and throw to first to start the relay around the bases.

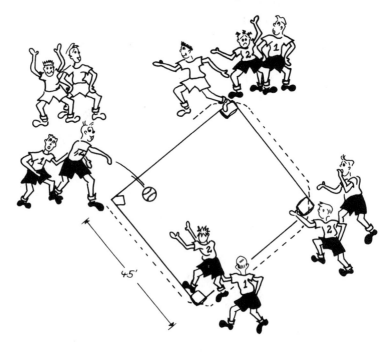

Players	6 on a team. Teams unlimited.
Equipment	Softballs and marked strike zones.
Area	Gymnasium or playground. (45 feet from target)
Skills	Pitching.
Game	The object is to see which team can pitch the greatest number of strikes. The teams line up single file behind their team captain, 45 feet from a strike zone marked on a wall. Each person takes one turn pitching underhand in an attempt to throw a strike. The player retrieves his own ball and throws it to the next player in line. He then goes to the rear of the line. The first team to pitch a predetermined number of strikes is declared the winner.
Scoring	One point is scored for each ball hitting the strike zone. The team scoring the most points is the winner.
Variations	A player is allowed to continue pitching until he misses.

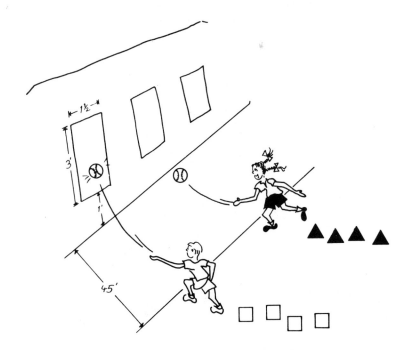

DANISH ROUNDERS

Players 8 on a team. Teams unlimited.

Equipment Tennis ball.

Area Playground or gymnasium. (45-foot bases)

Skills Throwing, catching, and base running.

Game The object is for batters to touch all bases and score a run without being put out. The pitcher throws the ball slightly above the head of the batter, who tries to hit the ball with his hand. Whether he hits the ball or not, he runs to first base and farther if possible. The fielding team returns the ball to the pitcher who downs the ball on the pitcher's mound. If the ball is downed before the runner reaches a base, he is out. Any number of players may be at a base at the same time, and on a strike or a hit they may or may not choose to run to the next base. When the ball is downed by the pitcher, any base runner off base is out. A caught fly ball puts out not only the batter, but also any players running between bases. Play is continued until all members have batted; then sides change.

Scoring One point is scored for each run.

Variations Use a stick bat.

KICK BALL

Players   8 on a team. Teams unlimited.

Equipment   Soccer ball.

Area   Gymnasium or playground. (35-foot bases)

Skills   Throwing, catching, fielding, and base running.

Game   The object is for the batter to score a run by kicking the ball. The game is played like softball with the following exceptions: the ball is rolled by the pitcher and kicked by the batter; no stealing is permitted.

Scoring   One point is scored each time a batter returns home safely.

Variations   (1) Have the batter place-kick, drop-kick, or punt the ball. (2) Use a volleyball, and have the batter bat a pitched ball with his fist or forearm. (3) Use a tennis ball, and have the pitcher bounce the ball once before the batter hits it with his hand. (4) Have the batter bounce the ball and hit it. (5) Have the batter use a volleyball serve.

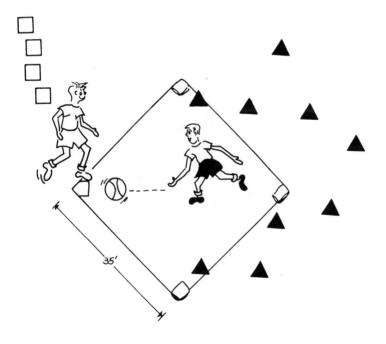

THROW SOFTBALL

Players   6 to 8 on a team. Teams unlimited.

Equipment   Softball.

Area   Playground or gymnasium. (45-foot bases)

Skills   Catching, throwing, fielding, and base running.

Game   The object is for the batter to run the bases without being put out. The game is played like softball except that the batter, instead of batting the ball, catches the pitched ball and immediately throws it into the field. The ball is then played as in regular softball. The batter is allowed only one throw per time at bat. If he drops a ball in the strike zone he is out. A foul ball is an out. There is no stealing.

Scoring   One point is scored for each run.

Variations   (1) Have the batter use an under-the-leg throw. (2) Use an underhand throw. (3) Use a batting tee.

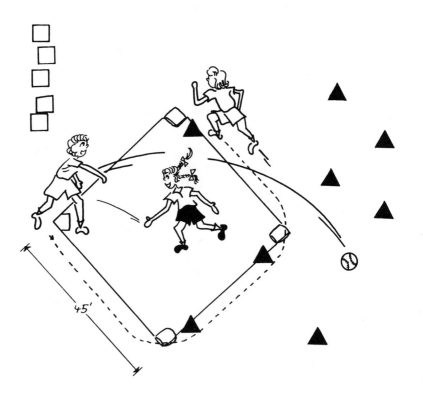

LINE BALL

Players   6 on a team. Teams unlimited.

Equipment   Softball and 2 bats.

Area   Playground or gymnasium. (Lines 30 feet apart)

Skills   Batting, fielding, and catching.

Game   The object is for the batter to drive a ground ball through the other team. Each team has a bat. The first player tosses the ball up and tries to bat it across the other team's goal line. The ball must hit the ground between the two lines. The other team tries to field the ball and then attempts to bat it back across the opponent's goal line. Each member of each team gets a chance to bat.

Scoring   One point is scored for each ball that crosses the other team's goal line.

Variations   Have players throw instead of bat the ball through the other team.

30′

BASE ON BALLS

Players	6 to 8 on a team. Teams unlimited.
Equipment	Softball and bat.
Area	Playground or gymnasium. (45-foot bases)
Skills	Catching, throwing, batting, and base running.
Game	The object is for the batter to hit the ball into fair territory and run the bases without stopping, before the catcher gains possession of the ball and calls "Stop." The batter throws the ball up, hits it into the field, and runs the bases. The fielders, instead of playing regular softball rules, throw the ball directly home to the catcher. There are no outs. A caught fly ball would mean no score. A foul ball would count as a turn at bat. After each batter has had a turn to bat, sides change.
Scoring	One point is scored for each base touched before the catcher receives the ball at home. A home run counts 4 points.
Variations	(1) Use a batting tee. (2) Have the batter throw the ball into the field instead of batting it. (3) Use a pitcher. (4) Instead of having the fielders throw the ball to the catcher, have them throw it to a pitcher, who must pitch a strike to stop the batter. Use a different pitcher for each batter. (5) Specify the number of throws in the relay.

TEAM PEPPER

Players	8 to 10 on a team. Teams unlimited.
Equipment	Softballs and bats.
Area	Playground or gymnasium.
Skills	Batting, pitching, and catching.
Game	The object is to see which team is most proficient in having each team member bat the ball to his teammates. Each team forms a circle with one member in the center of the circle with the bat. Each member in turn pitches the ball to the center player, and he in turn hits it to the person on the thrower's left. If it is missed, it must be replayed. This procedure continues on around the circle. After everyone has had a chance to bat, a round is completed.
Scoring	The team successfully finishing a round first is the winner.
Variations	Use other softball skills in this formation such as: batting and fielding ground balls, flyballs, and bunts.

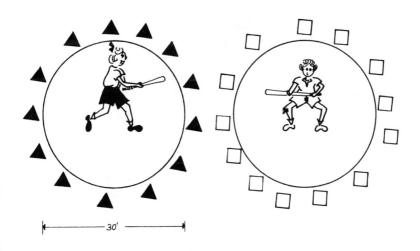

Players   6 to 8 on a team. Teams unlimited.

Equipment   Softball, 2 bats, 2 Indian clubs, and 2 bases for every two teams.

Area   Playground or gymnasium. (Bases 25 feet apart)

Skills   Batting, throwing, catching, and fielding.

Game   The object is for batters to score runs by hitting the ball and running to the opposite base before the Indian clubs can be knocked down by the fielders. There is a batter at each base. Two feet behind each base is an Indian club. The fielding team has a pitcher at each base, and the rest of the fielders are scattered around informally. There are no boundaries. The batters assume a position with the thick end of the bat touching the base. One of the pitchers throws the ball underhand at the Indian club from the opposite base. An out is scored every time a pin is knocked down. The batter attempts to protect the pin by hitting the ball. If he hits the ball in any direction, he quickly exchanges places with his teammate on the other base. The fielders try to recover the ball and knock down

the pins while the runners are exchanging places. If the
fielders do not succeed in knocking down pins in time, a
run is scored. The batters may exchange places any number of times on a hit and score a run on every exchange.
A player may knock down the pins by throwing the ball
at them any time the batter guarding the pins takes his
bat off the base. On the pitch, however, the bat on the
base is not a protection. A caught fly ball results in an
out. Pitchers are rotated after five pitches. The same two
batters continue to bat until an out is made. After an out
two new batters take over. Three outs retire a side.

Scoring One point is scored every time the batters exchange places.

Variations Allow a player only two bats or hits, after which he gives
up his place at bat to a teammate. After everyone has
batted, teams change sides.

HOME-RUN DERBY

Players   6 to 8 on a team. Teams unlimited.

Equipment   Softball and bat.

Area   Playground. (45-foot bases)

Skills   Batting, fielding, and catching.

Game   The object is for the batter to hit the ball safely over the restraining line. The restraining line is drawn from first to third base. A batted ball must travel over this line in order to be fielded. The infield area is between first, second, and third base and the restraining line. Each batter is given three successive chances (that is, three pitches by a pitcher from his own team) to hit the ball into fair territory across the restraining line. There is no base running. Only one player may field the ball. If the ball is fielded without an error, the batter is out. If the ball cannot be fielded or is fielded improperly, it is counted as a hit. Infielders and outfielders exchange positions each inning. Pitchers are changed each inning and are eligible to bat. When all the batters have had a turn, sides change.

Scoring   One point is scored for a hit in the infield. Two points for a hit in the outfield.

Variations   (1) Using a batting tee. (2) Have a batter throw up the ball himself and hit it. (3) Play by outs. (4) Let the team in the field furnish the pitcher.

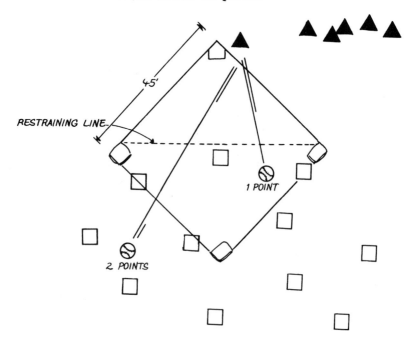

CIRCLE SOFTBALL

Players 6 to 8 on a team. Teams unlimited.

Equipment Softball and bat. (50-foot circle)

Area Playground or gymnasium.

Skills Batting, fielding, pitching, and catching.

Game The object is for the batting team to hit the ball out of a circle formed by the fielding team. The members of each team are numbered. The pitcher is the member of the fielding team whose number corresponds to that of the batter; thus each batter has a different pitcher. The fielders select a catcher to go into the circle. Each batter tries to hit five strike pitches out of the circle. The leader or umpire calls the strikes. After everyone has batted, sides change.

Scoring One point is scored for each batted ball that gets outside the circle.

Variations (1) Use a batting tee. (2) Adjust the size of the circle to the ability of the players. (3) Give batter only one try.

LONG BALL

Players	6 to 8 on a team. Teams unlimited.
Equipment	Softball and bat.
Area	Playground or gymnasium. (30 by 50 feet)
Skills	Pitching, catching, throwing, and batting.
Game	The object is for the batter to score a run by hitting the ball into fair territory and getting to far base and back home without being put out. The batter hits the pitched ball into fair territory and runs to the far base. He must reach the base before the ball or before he is tagged with the ball. He may stay there or try to return home. However, if he leaves the base, he cannot return except on a fly ball that is caught. Several runners may be on the far base as long as a batter is left. After all batters have had a chance to bat, sides change. First and third bases are used only to determine foul balls.
Scoring	One point is scored by each runner who returns to home plate safely.
Variations	(1) Play by outs. (2) Use a batting tee. (3) Have the players throw the ball or throw it up and hit it. (4) Place a mat midway between home and the far base and have the runner perform a stunt on his way to and from the far base, for example, a forward roll.

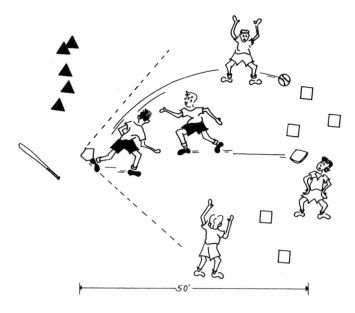

Players	8 to 10 on a team. Teams unlimited.
Equipment	Softball, bat, and 4 Indian clubs, tenpins, or milk cartons for every two teams.
Area	Playground or gymnasium. (45-foot bases)
Skills	Batting, catching, fielding, pitching, and throwing.
Game	The object is for the batter, after hitting the ball into fair territory, to circle the bases before the four pins can be knocked down in order by the fielders. The game is played like softball with the following exception: there is an Indian club on the outside corner of each base and in the middle of home plate. The pitcher throws the ball so that the batter can hit it. On a fair ball the batter circles outside the bases and touches home plate. In the meantime the fielders retrieve the ball and pass it in order to the first baseman, second, third, and to home. As the baseman receives the ball he knocks down the pin and throws to the next base. The batter is out (1) on a fly ball, (2) if he knocks down a pin, or (3) if the four pins can be knocked down by the fielders before he gets home. Rotate basemen after each inning. After all players on one side have batted, sides change.
Scoring	One point is scored by the batter if he beats the ball home.
Variations	(1) Play by outs. (2) Use the batting tee. (3) Adjust the number of pins and base lengths to the ability of players.

45'

Players   3 or more.

Equipment   Softball and bat.

Area   Playground. (45-foot base)

Skills   All the skills of softball.

Game   The object is for an individual to stay at bat as long as possible. There is only one base, first base. The batter must hit the ball into fair territory and run to first and back home before the ball can be returned to the catcher. If the batter is not put out before 5 runs are scored, the players automatically rotate. The rotation system goes like this: batter to right field, to center field, to left field, to third base, to shortstop, to second base, to first base, to pitcher, to catcher. The catcher becomes the next batter. A fly ball caught by a player puts him directly at bat. In this event the batter goes to the end of the rotation (right field), and the other players move up until the position of the fielder who caught the ball is filled.

Scoring   One point is scored for each run. The player with the most points wins.

Variations   (1) Use two batters (Two Old Cat), and allow the batter to stop at first base. (2) Use three batters and three bases. (3) Have the batter switch hit.

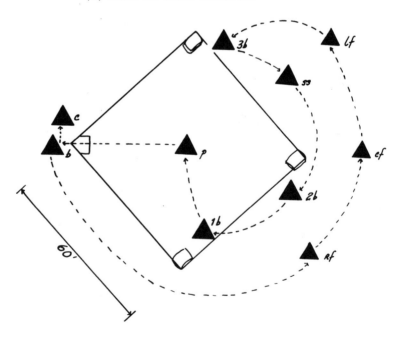

The following lead-up games, found elsewhere in this book, can easily be adapted to lead up to softball by substituting a softball and the softball skills one wishes to develop.

Battle Ball	163	Keep Away	19
Bombardment	7	Kick Over	145
Boundary Ball	143	Leader Ball	168
Circle Pass	71	Net Ball	162
Count Off	70	Newcomb	164
End Ball	13	Success	67
End Zone	144	Target Ball	24
Field Ball	21	Teacher Ball	93
Hit Away	34	Throw Around	68
Hit the Ball	147		

TOUCH FOOTBALL

Lead-up Games Designed to Develop Touch Football Skills [*]

Basic skills involved

Lead-up games	Ball handling	Lining up	Blocking	Ball carrying	Dodging	Tagging	Passing	Catching	Kicking	Centering	Covering
Over and under	X										
The line up		X									
Screening			X								
Fumble				X							
Open-field running				X	X						
Steal the football				X	X						
Boundary ball							X	X	X		
End zone							X	X			
Kick over								X	X		
Drop-kick contest								X	X		
Hit the ball							X	X			
Knock 'er down							X	X			X
Foot baseball							X	X	X	X	
Capture the football	X			X	X	X	X				
Goal ball	X						X	X			X
Field football	X						X	X	X		X
Kick-off football	X		X	X	X	X		X	X		
Pass ball	X		X	X	X	X	X	X			X
Flash ball	X	X	X	X	X	X	X	X	X	X	X
Aerial ball	X	X	X	X	X	X	X	X	X	X	X
Charge	C	O	N	D	I	T	I	O	N	I	N	G

---

[*] It is suggested that flags be used whenever tagging is part of the touch football lead-up games. The flags may be pieces of cloth tucked in the belt at the back of the player or they can be obtained commercially. Flags lessen body contact and make officiating easier, since there is no question whether or not the player has been tagged. The use of flags encourages more running than is generally characteristic of touch football.

Students should have many opportunities to play running and tagging games in the early grades, as a foundation for playing touch football. In addition, if a football can occasionally be substituted for a round ball in the games of low organization, ball-handling skills will be developed.

OVER AND UNDER

Players   6 to 8 on a team. Teams unlimited.

Equipment   Footballs.

Area   Playground or gymnasium.

Skills   Ball handling.

Game   The object is to see which team can be first to finish passing the ball over and under. Each player at the head of a team has a ball. The first player passes the ball over his head with both hands to the player behind him. This player passes the ball between his legs to the next player. The ball alternates over and under down the line. When the last player gets the ball, he runs to the front of the team and starts the over-and-under passing again. The ball has to be handed; it cannot be thrown.

Scoring   The team returning first to the original position wins.

Variations   (1) Have the ball passed only overhead or only underneath. (2) Have the end person weave through his team to get to the front of the line.

THE LINE-UP

Players 7 on a team. Teams unlimited.

Equipment Football.

Area Playground or gymnasium.

Skills Lining up.

Game The object is to see how quickly a team can line up on the line of scrimmage. Players line up beside each other in a crouching position, with one team right next to another. The leader takes a position near the middle of the line. The ball is on the ground in front of him. He picks up the ball, runs forward either straight or on a diagonal, and places the ball on the ground. Members of the teams charge forward as the ball is picked up and line up again when the ball is placed on the ground.

Scoring The team whose members first form a straight line in crouched position with no players offside is declared the winner.

Variations None.

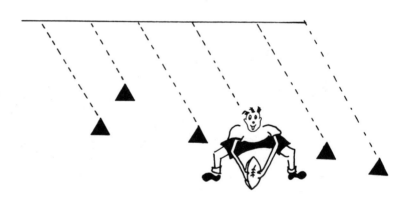

SCREENING

Players	Any number.
Equipment	None.
Area	Playground or gymnasium.
Skills	Charging and blocking.
Game	The object is for one team to prevent the other from breaking through its line. One team is designated as blockers, the other as chargers. On a signal the chargers attempt to break through the blockers' line, while the blockers attempt to hold them out. After a count of five, play is stopped. The number of chargers who successfully break through the line are counted. The teams then reverse their roles.
Scoring	The team with the greatest number of players breaking through is the winner.
Variations	None.

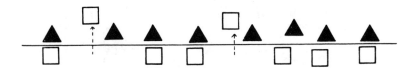

FUMBLE

Players   6 to 8 on a team. Teams unlimited.

Equipment   Football.

Area   Playground or gymnasium.

Skills   Carrying the ball.

Game   The object is for players on one team to carry the ball through the other team without having it knocked from their hands. Members of one team make a lane by forming two facing lines about 3 feet apart. Members of the other team, one at a time, run down the lane carrying the ball. Line players try to dislodge or jar the ball free or cause the runner to fumble. The use of feet by either team is illegal.

Scoring   The team with the most runners carrying the ball through successfully is the winner.

Variations   Have the runners weave in and out among the line players changing the ball from arm to arm as they run.

Players   6 to 8 on a team. Teams unlimited.

Equipment   Flags.

Area   Playground or gymnasium. (30 by 60 yards)

Skills   Dodging and tagging.

Game   The object is for players to cross the field without losing their flags. One team runs across the field while the other team tries to detach the runners' flags. Teams alternate running.

Scoring   The team with the most runners who get through without losing their flags is the winner.

Variations   Have only a few players with flags; the others serve as blockers.

STEAL THE FOOTBALL

Players 6 to 8 on a team. Teams unlimited.

Equipment Football.

Area Playground or gymnasium. (40 feet between lines)

Skills Dodging and tagging.

Game The object is for a player to get the football back to his goal line without being tagged by an opponent. Each member of each team has a number. When a number is called, the opposing players having that number rush to get the ball.

Scoring The player who returns the ball to his goal line without being tagged scores 1 point for his team.

Variations (1) Call out several numbers. Allow the players to lateral and pass the ball. (2) Increase the distance between teams.

BOUNDARY BALL

Players	8 to 10 on a team. Teams unlimited.
Equipment	Footballs.
Area	Playground or gymnasium. (40 by 60 feet)
Skills	Passing, catching, and kicking.
Game	The object is for players to pass or kick the ball over their opponent's goal line while remaining in their own half of the field. Players try to prevent balls from crossing their goal line. Balls are thrown or kicked back and forth. Players may take the ball to the center line before throwing or kicking it. Each player securing the ball must throw or kick it himself and not give it to a teammate. (This rule is to prevent the more highly skilled from monopolizing the game.)
Scoring	Each ball that rolls or bounces over a goal line scores 1 point. Balls going across a goal line on the fly score 2 points.
Variations	(1) Players may not move with the ball, but may pass it to a teammate who is in a more advantageous position. (2) Use more balls to increase the participation and activity.

40' X 60'

Players   6 to 8 on a team. Teams unlimited.

Equipment   Footballs.

Area   Playground or gymnasium. (40 by 60 feet)

Skills   Throwing and catching.

Game   The object is to throw the ball on the fly into the opponent's end zone. Players may not enter the end zones except to retrieve a dead ball. Players must stay in their half of the field. Each team should have at least two footballs to start the game.

Scoring   One point is scored for each ball thrown on the fly into the end zone.

Variations (1) Kick instead of pass. (2) End ball is a good variation of this game. (3) Use more balls.

KICK OVER

Players   6 to 8 on a team. Teams unlimited.

Equipment   Football.

Area   Playground. (30 by 60 yards)

Skills   Kicking and catching.

Game   The object is for players to kick the ball over the opponent's goal line without its being caught. The ball is put in play at a point halfway between one team's goal line and the center line. If a player catches a kick on the fly, he is allowed five steps forward, from which point he kicks the ball as far toward the opponent's goal line as possible. If the ball is not caught, it is kicked from the point where it was first touched. A ball caught behind the goal line is brought to the goal line, where five steps are taken. The team scored upon puts the ball in play from a point halfway to the center line. The kicking team must be behind the kicker. The receiving team may be no closer than 30 feet from the kicker.

Scoring   One point is scored for each uncaught ball that is kicked over the opponent's goal line.

Variations   (1) Pass instead of kick. (2) Use different kinds of kicks.

30 X 60 YARDS

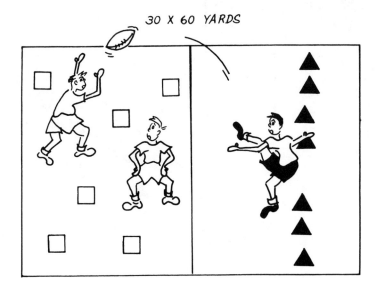

DROP-KICK CONTEST

Players 6 to 8 on a team. Teams unlimited.

Equipment Footballs and a goal.

Area Playground.

Skills Kicking and catching.

Game The object is to kick field goals. Teams alternate kicking on successive kicks. The ball must be drop-kicked or place-kicked from beyond a 10-yard line. All team members must have a turn kicking. Each player tries to kick the ball over the crossbar and between the goal posts. Opponents try to catch a successfully kicked ball.

Scoring One point is scored for each successful kick, and if opponents fail to catch the kicked ball an additional point is earned.

Variations (1) More points for a longer kick. (2) Pass instead of kick.

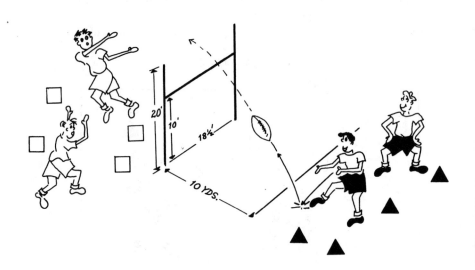

HIT THE BALL

Players	6 to 8 on a team. Teams unlimited.
Equipment	Football and basketball.
Area	Playground or gymnasium. (30 feet between lines)
Skills	Throwing for accuracy and catching.
Game	The object is to hit a target ball with a football. The leader in the center of the field tosses a basketball straight up into the air. While the ball is still in the air, a player from one team throws the football at it. The members of the other team must stand behind their end line until the ball is thrown at the target ball; then they run forward and try to catch the football in the air. The teams then switch roles for the next throw. Each player eventually has a turn throwing at the target ball.
Scoring	The team hitting the target ball the greatest number of times is the winner.
Variations	(1) Use several balls. (2) Use different kinds of target balls, for example, a cage ball. (3) Leave the target ball on the ground. Each team has several balls. Object is to force the target ball over the opponent's goal line by hitting it with a football. The football must be thrown from behind the goal line and the target ball can only be stopped by a thrown ball.

KNOCK 'ER DOWN

Players	6 to 8 on a team. Teams unlimited.
Equipment	Footballs.
Area	Playground or gymnasium. (40 by 60 feet)
Skills	Passing, catching, and covering.
Game	The object is for team members on one side of the neutral zone to pass the ball over the neutral zone to their teammates. Opposing team members attempt to intercept or knock down the ball. A ball on the ground is a free ball. A ball going out of bounds is given to the team that did not lose possession of it. An out-of-bounds ball cannot be passed directly over the neutral zone.
Scoring	Each completed pass across the neutral zone counts 1 point.
Variations	Use more than one ball at a time.

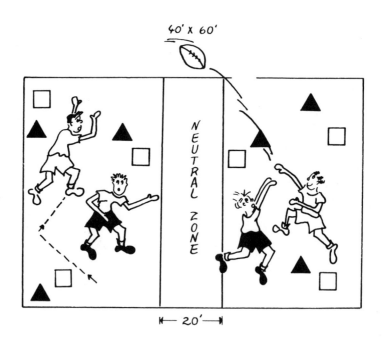

Players   8 to 10 on a team. Teams unlimited.

Equipment   Football.

Area   Playground or gymnasium. (45-foot bases)

Skills   Centering, kicking, passing, and catching.

Game   The object is for the batter to kick a football without having it blocked and score a run as in baseball. The batter stands at home plate, and the pitcher (a member of his own team) centers the ball to him. The batter kicks the ball into the field. The ball must go beyond the short kick line, a line running from first to third base. Two members of the fielding team stationed behind the short line may rush the batter as the pitcher centers the ball. After the batter kicks the ball, he runs the bases as in baseball. The batter is out (1) if the rushers block the kick, (2) if the kicked ball is caught on the fly. Otherwise the game is played like baseball.

Scoring   Each batter who gets home scores 1 point for his team.

Variations   Have someone place the ball in position for the batter to place kick.

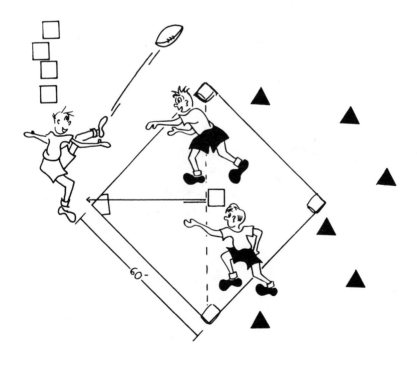

CAPTURE THE FOOTBALL

Players	8 to 10 on a team. Teams unlimited.
Equipment	2 footballs.
Area	Playground. (30 by 60 yards)
Skills	Running, dodging, throwing, and catching.
Game	The object is for one team to get the opponent's football back to its own half of the field without being tagged. The game starts with each team lined up along the center line and each ball centered on opposite goal lines. On a signal, some of the players attempt to capture the football while the others stay back to defend. The ball may be advanced by either running or passing. Any player touched by an opponent in the opponent's half of the field must go into prison, and the ball is downed at that point and cannot be advanced until the prisoner is freed. The prison is a designated area on each goal line. The ball cannot be touched as long as the offensive team has prisoners. Prisoners can be freed by one of their own players running into the prison without being touched. When freed, a player along with the person freeing him must return to their own half of the field before going for the ball. If a ball is dropped when passed or lateraled, it goes back to the spot where it was thrown.
Scoring	A team wins by getting the opponent's football back to its own half of the field or by advancing it closest to the center line.
Variations	None.

Players	8 to 10 on a team. Teams unlimited.
Equipment	Basketball backboards and football.
Area	Playground or gymnasium. (30 by 60 yards)
Skills	Passing for accuracy, catching, and covering.
Game	The object is for one team to hit the opponent's backboard (or other similar goal) with the football and to prevent the opponent from hitting its backboard. The game is started by a kickoff from the center of the field. From then on the game is played like keep away (p. 19), with this exception: no one may advance toward the goal while in possession of the ball. The player with the ball may move only in a lateral or backward direction. No player is allowed to make personal contact with an opponent. After an unsuccessful try for a goal, the defensive team is given possession of the ball behind its own goal line. A goal cannot be scored directly on a throw-in from out of bounds. After a goal is scored, the team scored on kicks off.
Scoring	Two points are scored by hitting the opponent's backboard or goal with the football.
Variations	Have a scoring scale depending on how far away from the goal a hit is made.

30' X 60' YARDS

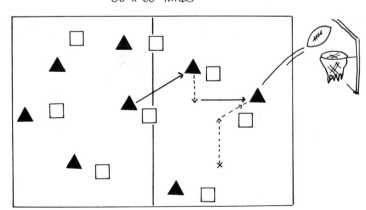

FIELD FOOTBALL

Players   8 to 10 on a team. Teams unlimited.

Equipment   Football and soccer goals.

Area   Playground. (30 by 60 yards)

Skills   Kicking, passing, and catching.

Game   The object is to pass the football through the opponent's goal. The game is played like field ball (p. 21) except that a football is used. The game begins with a kickoff from midfield. The ball is advanced by passing or kicking. There is no running with the ball except by the goalkeeper in the penalty area. A player is not allowed to hold the ball longer than 3 seconds. Guarding is permitted as in basketball.

Scoring   A ball passed through the goal from outside the penalty area scores 2 points. One point for a goal made from within the penalty area.

Variations   None.

30 X 60 YARDS

Players 6 to 8 on a team. Teams unlimited.

Equipment Football.

Area Playground. (30 by 60 yards)

Skills Kicking, catching, dodging, and tagging.

Game The object is to return the kickoff as far as possible without being tagged. One team kicks off as in regular touch football from the center of the field. The player receiving the ball returns it up the field as far as he can without being tagged by an opponent. To avoid being tagged, the ball carrier may use a lateral pass to another player on his team, who may continue on down the field, but he may not use the forward pass. Team members may screen for him. When the ball carrier is tagged, the ball is dead. The other team then kicks off from the middle of the field.

Scoring The team advancing farthest up the field is the winner.

Variations None.

30 X 60 YARDS

FLASH BALL

Players 6 to 8 on a team. Teams unlimited.

Equipment Football.

Area Playground. (30 by 60 yards)

Skills Passing, catching, kicking, dodging, and tagging.

Game The object is to carry the ball over the opponent's goal line or to pass to a teammate who is over the goal line. The game is started with a kickoff from midfield. The offensive team is allowed four downs to score. The ball may be passed from any place at any time. The defensive team must line up 5 yards away from the ball except when the offensive team is less than 5 yards from the goal line. In this event the defensive team can line up on the line of scrimmage. All other rules are those of touch football.

Scoring A touchdown scores 6 points.

Variations (1) The offensive team rotates one position clockwise after each play. (2) No huddle is permitted, to speed up play. (3) The offensive team loses possession of the ball on every incompleted pass or fumble. (4) The field is divided into four equal zones. Each team has four downs to move from one zone to another.

30 X 60 YARDS

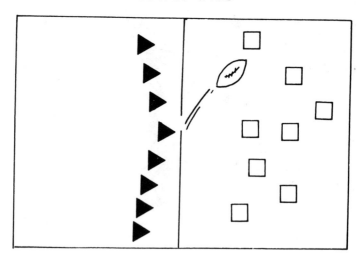

Players	8 to 10 on a team. Teams unlimited.
Equipment	Tied rolled mat, cage ball, or some other bulky object.
Area	Playground or gymnasium. (40 by 60 feet)
Skills	Conditioning.
Game	The object is to advance the rolled mat from the center of the area over the opponent's goal line. The game starts with both teams lined up on their own goal line. On a signal both teams rush for the mat placed equidistant between goal lines and attempt to move it to the opposite goal. There are no rules except that unnecessary roughness is prohibited.
Scoring	The team getting the mat over the opponent's goal line, or closest to it, wins.
Variations	None.

The following lead-up games, found elsewhere in this book, can easily be adapted to lead up to touch football by substituting a football and the football skills one wishes to develop.

Around the Horn	118	Kick Ball	121
Base on Balls	124	Leader Ball	168
Battle Ball	163	Long Pass	65
Bombardment	7	Mickey Mouse	92
Bull in the Ring	10	Newcomb	164
Circle Pass	71	On the Whistle	61
Circle Target	11	Overtake Throw	114
Count Off	70	Star Lacrosse	72
Dodging and Tackling	42	Teacher Ball	93
End Ball	13	Twist	62
Hit Away	34	Zig-Zag Throw	117
Keep Away	19		

VOLLEYBALL

Lead-up Games Designed to Develop Volleyball Skills

Lead-up game	Basic skills involved						
	Throwing	Catching	Volleying	Setting up	Serving	Blocking	Spiking
Hot potato	X	X					
Mass deck tennis	X	X					
Net ball	X	X					
Battle ball	X	X					
Newcomb	X	X					
One-bounce volleyball			X		X		
Fabric volleyball			X	X	X	X	X
Leader ball			X	X			
Zig-zag volley			X				
Target ball					X		
Keep it up			X				
Pass placement			X	X			
Backboard set-up			X	X			
Volleyball, modified			X	X	X		
Spike and block			X	X		X	X
Two-, three-, or four-man volleyball			X	X	X	X	X
Three-pass volleyball			X	X	X	X	X

HOT POTATO

Players 8 to 10 players in a group.

Equipment Volleyball or bean bag.

Area Playroom, classroom, playing field, or gymnasium.

Skills Throwing, catching, and accuracy in passing.

Game The players sit in a circle. One player who is selected to be "it" assumes a position in the center of the circle. The object of the game is to prevent the player in the center of the circle from catching the "hot potato." The player seated in the circle starts the game by throwing the hot potato to another player. The hot potato is thrown rapidly in any direction, while "it" is attempting to intercept the ball. When the ball is intercepted, the player responsible goes into the center of the circle and becomes "it."

Variations (1) The hot potato may be thrown clockwise or counterclockwise. (2) The player holding it when a whistle signal is given has a point scored against him. (3) More than one hot potato may be used. (4) Players may volley the hot potato rather than catch it.

MASS DECK TENNIS

Players   10 to 40. Players are divided into two equal teams and placed on the court as for volleyball.

Equipment   A deck tennis ring made of pliable rubber or a ring 6 inches in diameter made of rope; two standards; a badminton net 5 feet or 7½ feet high.

Area   Playground or gymnasium. (Court 30 by 60 feet)

Skills   Throwing and catching with either hand. Volleyball rules.

Game   The object of the game is to throw the ring back and forth over the net in an effort to prevent the opposing team's returning it. The ring must be caught with one hand, either left or right, and must be returned with the same hand. The ring must be thrown with an upward stroke, for a down stroke is a foul either on service or in a rally.

30' X 60'

SERVICE: The server, standing outside of the right-hand court, tries to throw the ring with an upward toss beyond the neutral area and into the diagonally opposite half court. If the serving team scores the point, the ring is thrown again by the server from the left-hand court. The server continues to alternate from left to right courts until his side makes an error or a foul.

RALLY: Following service, the ring is thrown back and forth over the net until a player misses or fouls. If the serving side misses or fouls, no point is made, but the serving side loses the serve. If an opponent misses or fouls, 1 point is awarded to the serving team. The neutral area is disregarded except for service.

FOULS: Catching the ring with both hands; changing the ring from the catching hand in order to throw more successfully; while serving, stepping on or over the end line; making a downward stroke when throwing the ring; permitting the ring to touch any part of the body other than the hand.

Scoring The serving side scores 1 point whenever the receiving side misses a play or makes a foul. A game consists of 15 points. If a game reaches 14 all, one team must score 2 successive points in order to win. A match consists of two out of three games.

Variations None.

NET BALL

Players	Unlimited.
Equipment	Volleyball or rubber ball and net.
Area	Gymnasium or playing field. (Court 30 by 60 feet)
Skills	Catching and throwing.
Game	The object of the game is to throw the ball back and forth over the net until a player on one side fails to return it, allows it to touch the floor, causes it to go out of bounds, or walks with it. A net is stretched across the width of the field or court dividing it into two equal courts. The players are placed in two or three lines across the court, the number in each line depending upon the number playing. The player in the back right-hand corner serves the ball by pitching or throwing it across the net into the opponent's half of the court. The ball is then caught by the receiving team and must be returned by pitch or throw by the same player. The play should be lively, as each team scores only on its opponent's failure to catch the ball.
Scoring	Scores are made by serving side only; if the serving side fails to return the ball or fouls, the opposing team receives the service. Twenty-one points constitute a game.
Variations	Cover net with sheet to conceal the direction and timing of the returning ball.

30' X 60'

BATTLE BALL

Players	Unlimited.
Equipment	An odd number of volleyballs or similar-sized rubber balls (at least 7).
Area	Playground, playing field, or gymnasium.
Skills	Throwing and catching.
Game	Divide the players into two equal teams. The object of the game is to throw the balls over the net as quickly as possible, so that when the time limit has expired there will be as many balls as possible in possession of the other team. At the beginning of the game the balls are divided, one side having one extra. The game is played in 3-minute quarters. Four quarters constitute a game. Teams exchange sides of court at half time.
Scoring	At the end of each quarter the balls are counted; this count represents the score. The team with the lower number of points at the end of the fourth quarter is the winner.
Variations	None.

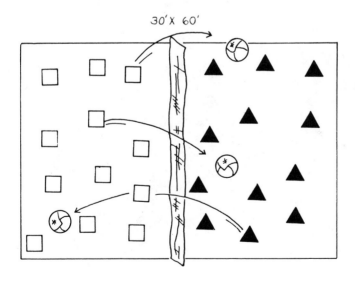

30' X 60'

NEWCOMB

Players Unlimited. Players divided into sets of equal teams. 9 to 12 players on a team make a good game.

Equipment Volleyball net placed at regulation height. Volleyball, soccerball, basketball, or playground ball.

Area Regulation volleyball court. The size may be adjusted to the number of players.

Skills Throwing and catching.

Game The object of the game is to throw the ball over the net so that it strikes the floor within the opponent's court and to catch and return ball thrown back by the opponents. Players are lined up as for volleyball, and the serve is taken in the same order, starting at the back right-hand corner. The server starts the play by tossing the ball over the net. Receivers attempt to catch the ball and throw it back.

30' X 60'

A point is made for one team when: (1) the ball drops to the floor of the opponent's court; (2) an opponent causes the ball to go into or under the net; (3) one or more on the serving team touches the served ball before it goes over the net; and (4) an opponent throws the ball out of bounds, provided it is not touched by a member of the opposing team. (If a player touches a ball, he is responsible for catching it and may not claim that it was going out of bounds.)

Any player on the team may catch the ball and may either throw it back across the net or may pass it to a teammate who then throws it over. Fouls are: holding the ball more than 3 seconds; running with the ball; stepping over the service line; touching net while ball is in play.

Scoring Scoring rules differ from volleyball in that 1 point is scored every time the ball strikes the floor; that is, either serving or receiving sides may score. Play continues until the ball drops on one side of the net. If the serving side lets the ball drop on its side or fails to make a good serve, it is side out, and the other team rotates and starts serving. The server is not allowed help on the serve. The team scoring 15 points first wins the game.

Variations Volley newcomb. Serve as in volleyball, play as in newcomb.

Players   10 to 20.

Equipment   Volleyball and volleyball net.

Area   Volleyball court. (30 by 60 feet, with the top of the net 6½ feet from the ground)

Skills   Serving, volleying, rotation.

Game   Players divide into two teams, one team on either side of the net. The first player on the serving team serves the ball from behind the service line into the opposite court. The server has two trials to make a good serve. If he succeeds, he continues to serve until he fails to make a good serve or until his team fails to return the ball to opponent's court. Then the side is out and opponents serve. After side out, players rotate positions (see illustration). Each time the ball crosses the net it must bounce once in court before it is returned. No player may hit the ball more than once before another player hits it, but any number of players may hit.

Fouls: Failure to make a good serve in two trials; striking ball on return before it has bounced once; allowing ball to bounce more than once; player hitting ball more than once in succession; hitting ball with fist; failure to return ball over net; out-of-bounds ball.

Scoring   Team scores 1 point for each successful serve that opponents fail to return. Fifteen points constitute a game.

Variations   None.

30' X 60'

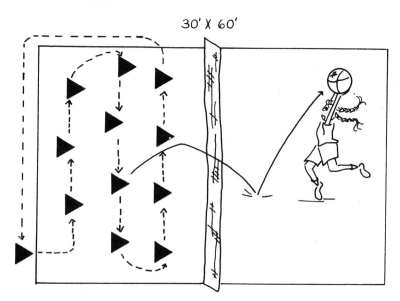

Players	4 to 40.
Equipment	Volleyball net; rope or wire mesh may be used as a net. A lightweight material may be fashioned into a ball, for example, sponge, wool, rags, or plastic. Shape the material until the circumference is approximately the same size as a regulation volleyball.
Area	Volleyball court with the dimensions adjusted to number and age of players. Gymnasium or playing field.
Skills	Serving, overhand volleying, underhand volleying, spiking, recovering ball from the net, blocking. Useful in teaching volleyball rules.
Game	Divide the players into equal teams, as in volleyball. Like a volleyball, the fabric ball is played with the hands. Volleyball rules are used. The ball is put into play at the back right-hand corner. A player may not play the ball twice in succession.
Scoring	The same scoring is used as in volleyball. Only the serving team may score points. If the serving team fails to make a legal service, fails to return the ball over the net, or sends the ball out of bounds, the opposing team becomes the serving team.
Variations	Beach ball, cage ball.

30' X 60'

LEADER BALL

Players   8 to 10 on a team. Teams unlimited.

Equipment Volleyballs (1 for each team).

Area   Gymnasium or playing field.

Skills   Volleying, tapping, and setting up.

Game   The object of the game is for each player to tap the ball with accuracy to the leader. The players are divided into equal teams in straight lines. The leader stands facing his team, 10 feet away. The leader tosses the ball into the air and taps it to the first player in his line, who immediately taps the ball back to the leader. Players are encouraged to tap the ball with the fingers of both hands. When the first player has tapped the ball back to the leader, he moves to the end of his line. When the first player returns to his original position, a round is completed. There is no penalty for the ball's touching the floor or ground; the loss of time is sufficient penalty.

Scoring   Five points for first place, 3 points for second place, and 1 point for third place. Points are awarded at the end of each round. A round is completed when a new player becomes the leader. The team with the greatest number of points at the end of the final round is the winner.

Variations Substitute various types of passes.

ZIG-ZAG VOLLEY

Players   20 to 100.

Equipment   Rubber ball or volleyball.

Area   Playground or gymnasium.

Skills   Overhead volleying, underhand volleying, accuracy in passing.

Game   The players are divided into two or more teams, which compete against each other. Each team is divided into two facing ranks, the players standing side by side with a distance of 2 to 4 feet between them. The ranks are 3 feet apart. The two ranks are staggered so that each player is opposite a space instead of a player.

The first player in one rank of each team has a ball. At a given signal he tosses the ball into the air and hits it with both hands to the first player in the opposite rank. This player taps it with the fingers to the second player of the first rank, and so on, in zig-zag form to the end of the line, where the ball is immediately sent back again in the same way to the front. The group that first gets its ball back to the head of the line wins.

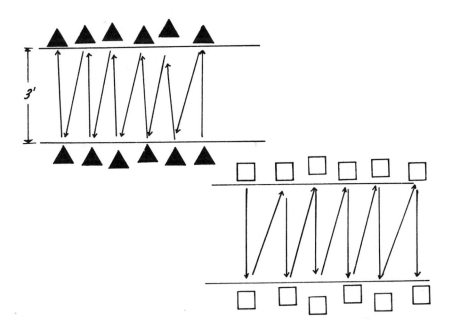

170 *Scoring* Five points for first place, 3 points for second place, 2 points for third place, 1 point for fourth place. The team with the greatest number of points at the end of playing time is the winner.

Variations Two or more balls may be used. Start the second ball down the line as soon as the first ball has reached the third player. When several balls are used in this way, the last player of the line must hold the balls until all are received before starting them on their return journey.

TARGET BALL

Players	6 to 10 players on a team. Teams unlimited.
Equipment	Volleyballs and one wall with approximately 30- or 40-foot approach. One target for each team is placed on the wall.
Area	Gymnasium, playground area, tennis backboard.
Skills	Volleyball serving for placement.
Game	Each team stands behind the pitching line, which is 30 to 40 feet from the target. Using an underhand service, each player on a team serves the ball to the target.
Scoring	If the server hits the numbered area, he gets the number shown in that area. If the ball hits the line, no points are scored. The team first reaching a predetermined number of points, or the team that has the highest total of points, wins the game.
Variations	As the skill of the players develops, the sidearm or overhead service may be used.

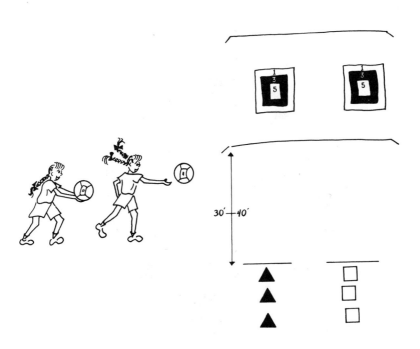

KEEP IT UP

Players	Unlimited. Teams form large circles.
Equipment	1 volleyball per team.
Area	Gymnasium or playing field.
Skills	Overhand and underhand volleying.
Game	On signal a team member tosses ball into air. Players, using both hands, keep striking it up into the air. The team that keeps the ball up longest wins 1 point. A player may not hit the ball twice in succession.
Scoring	Team that makes most points at end of playing period is winner.
Variations	Each contact made with the ball may score 1 point. The team with the greatest number of points is the winner. Each circle may play separately, attempting to score higher than the previous circle.

Players	8 players on a team. Teams unlimited.
Equipment	Volleyballs (1 for each team), a net, and 2 standards.
Area	Playground, playing field, or gymnasium.
Skills	Controlling ball and placing passes.
Game	Divide the eight players on each team in half, four on either side of the net. Number the teams 1, 2, 3, 4, etc. To start the game, A of team 1 tosses the ball to H of his own team, H volleys to B, B volleys to G, etc. The ball is passed up and down the line so long as the ball does not touch the floor; the ball must be passed to the proper player as well. If the ball should touch the floor or if it is not passed to the next player in line, the ball is dead. Team 2 then moves to the net to begin its game. This team is attempting to score more points and complete a greater number of passes than team 1. Continue until each team has had an opportunity at the net.
Scoring	Each successful pass scores 1 point.
Variations	None.

30' X 60'

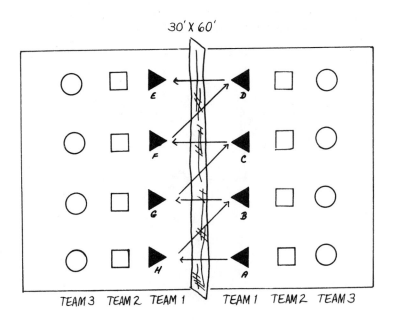

TEAM 3   TEAM 2   TEAM 1   TEAM 1   TEAM 2   TEAM 3

BACKBOARD SET-UP

Players Unlimited. The number of basketball backboards would determine the number of players.

Equipment 1 basketball backboard and 1 volleyball for each squad. Wall may be substituted for backboard.

Area Gymnasium or outdoor court.

Skills Receiving and passing for accuracy.

Game The object of the game is to see which squad can hit the backboard the most times using a legal volleyball pass. The leader for each squad, who stands under the backboard, tosses the ball up and volleys to the first player in line, who makes a high pass in an attempt to hit the backboard. In turn, each player in line receives a volley from the leader. The team with the greatest number of points after a specific number of rounds is the winner. The leader should be changed after each round. Each squad forms a line approximately 10 feet in front of the backboard.

Scoring One point is scored each time a player hits the backboard with a legal pass. The ball may be played with the hands or forearms.

Variations Two points may be scored if the player passes the ball through the basket.

Players   12 to 24.

Equipment   Net, 6½ feet from the floor; large ball or volleyball.

Area   A volleyball court modified in size for the number playing.

Skills   Two-hand volleying, assisting, setting up, and serving.

Game   The object of the game is to volley the ball back and forth over the net in an effort to prevent the opposing team's returning it. The ball must be clearly batted. Six, nine, or twelve players form a team. They are arranged in lines of three or four on each side of the net. A regulation volleyball game is played, with the following modifications in the rules: (1) the server may serve from a position in the center of the court; (2) two or more service trials may be allowed. An assist on the serve is permissible, which means that a teammate may play a ball that has been served in an effort to help it over the net; (3) during the rally there is no limit to the number of players who may play the ball before it goes over the net; (4) the ball may be hit not more than twice in succession by the same player; (5) the rotation of playing positions may be eliminated; (6) the ball may be played from a bounce instead of from the air.

Scoring   Scores are made by opponent's failure to return the ball. Only the serving side scores. Fifteen or 21 points may constitute a game.

Variations   Progress to regulation volleyball by eliminating some of the modified rules.

30' X 60'

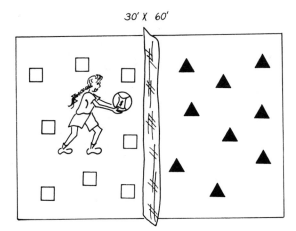

SPIKE AND BLOCK

Players   8 to 10 players on a team. Teams unlimited.

Equipment   Volleyball and net.

Area   Regulation volleyball court. Lower the net to 6½ feet for girls, and gradually raise to 7½ feet when spike is learned.

Skills   Passing, setting up, spiking, and blocking.

Game   Teams line up in file formation facing the net. Team 1 is the offensive team and team 2 the defensive team. When each player on team 1 has had an opportunity to spike the ball, and each player on team 2 an opportunity to block the spike, the teams exchange positions. Player C passes the ball to player A, who sets up the ball. Player B takes his run to spike. The first player on the defensive team times the movement of the ball to attempt a block on the play. Illustration shows the movements of the players as they rotate clockwise.

Scoring   A successful spike, that is, a ball that is not blocked by the defensive team, scores 1 point. A successful block, that is, a blocked ball that returns to the offensive side of the net, also scores 1 point. When all members of both teams have had an opportunity to spike and block, an inning is completed. Five innings constitute a game. The team with the highest number of points at the end of five innings is the winner.

Variations   None.

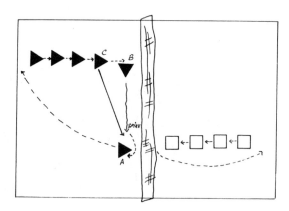

TWO-, THREE-, OR FOUR-MAN VOLLEYBALL

Players   2, 3, or 4 players on a team.

Equipment   Volleyball and volleyball net.

Area   Indoor or outdoor court. (30 by 60 feet. Court size may be reduced for beginning players)

Skills   All volleyball skills.

Game   The game is played exactly like volleyball with fewer players. This version encourages more active play and develops individual skills more rapidly.

Scoring   Regular volleyball scoring. Games of shorter duration are recommended for larger groups.

Variations   (1) Encourage players to change the direction of their passes, or insist on three volleys per side. (2) Game may be played with a time limit; the team with the highest score at the end of playing time wins the game.

30' X 60'

THREE-PASS VOLLEYBALL

Players 6 to 24.

Equipment Volleyball net and volleyball.

Area Regulation volleyball court.

Skills Controlling ball, setting up for spiking, and spiking.

Game The object of this game is to instill in players the idea of using a pass and a set-up for a spike instead of hitting the ball back over the net the first time. Regulation volleyball rules are used with the exception that a team loses the point or serve if the first or second player returns the ball over the net. Each team must take its full three plays on the ball each time. If the ball goes over the net on the first or second impetus, play is immediately stopped, and the point or serve is awarded to the opponent.

Scoring Regulation scoring rules are observed with the previously mentioned exception. Fifteen or 21 points constitute a game.

Variations Spiking as the only method of scoring.

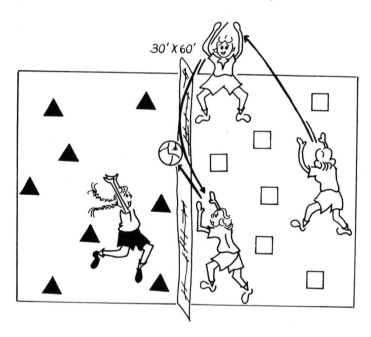

30' X 60'

The technique of striking a ball with the hands and forearms is unique to the game of volleyball. Therefore, most of the other lead-up games in this text are not adaptable. The authors would like to suggest the following skill tests, which are suitable for game situations:

Volleyball Service Test   Spike Test
Wall Volley Test   Block Test
Set-Up Test   Recovery from Net

These can be found in the *Selected Volleyball Articles* and *Beginning Volleyball* publications which are listed under Selected References.

General

DeWitt, R. T., *Teaching Individual and Team Sports*. Englewood Cliffs, N.J.: Prentice-Hall, Inc., 1953.

Frymir, Alice W. and Marjorie Hillas, *Team Sports for Women*. New York: A. S. Barnes & Co., 1942.

Meyer, M. H. and M. M. Schwarz, *Team Sports for Women*. Philadelphia: W. B. Saunders Co., 1957.

Miller, D. M. and K. L. Ley, *Individual and Team Sports for Women*. Englewood Cliffs, N.J.: Prentice-Hall, Inc., 1955.

Paterson, Ann, ed., *Team Sports for Girls*. New York: The Ronald Press Company, 1958.

Pearson, George B., *Methods of Teaching the Fundamental Skills of Team Sports*. Dubuque, Iowa: William C. Brown Company, Publishers, 1960.

Shaw, John H., ed., *Selected Team Sports for Men*. Philadelphia: W. B. Saunders Co., 1952.

Vannier, Maryhelen and Hally B. Poindexter, *Individual and Team Sports for Girls and Women*. Philadelphia: W. B. Saunders Co., 1960.

Basketball

Basketball Instructors Guide. Chicago: The Athletic Institute, 1961.

Bee, Clair and Ken Norton, *Drills and Fundamentals*. New York: The Ronald Press Company.

Bunn, John W., *The Basketball Coach: Guides to Success*. Englewood Cliffs, N.J.: Prentice-Hall, Inc., 1961.

Cooke, David C., *Better Basketball for Boys*. New York: Dodd, Mead & Co., 1960.

Dean, Everett S., *Progressive Basketball: Methods and Philosophy*. Englewood Cliffs, N.J.: Prentice-Hall, Inc., 1950.

Hutton, Joe and Vern B. Hoffman, *Basketball*. Mankato, Minn.: Creative Educational Society, Inc., 1961.

Lai, William T., *Winning Basketball*. Englewood Cliffs, N.J.: Prentice-Hall, Inc., 1955.

Lawrence, Helen B. and Grace I. Fox, *Basketball for Girls and Women*. New York: McGraw-Hill Book Company, 1954.

Meissner, Wilhelmine and Elizabeth Meyers, *Basketball for Girls* (rev. ed.). New York: The Ronald Press Company, 1952.

Newell, Pete and John Bennington, *Basketball Methods*. New York: The Ronald Press Company, 1962.

Official Basketball Guide. Washington, D.C.: The Division for Girls and Women's Sports, American Association for Health, Physical Education, and Recreation (published annually).

Pinholster, Garland F., *Encyclopedia of Basketball Drills.* Englewood Cliffs, N.J.: Prentice-Hall, Inc., 1958.

Selected Basketball Articles. Washington, D.C.: The Division for Girls and Women's Sports, American Association for Health, Physical Education, and Recreation (published annually).

Teague, Bertha Frank, *Basketball for Girls.* New York: The Ronald Press Company, 1962.

V-Five Association of America, *Basketball* (2nd ed.). Annapolis, Md.: United States Naval Institute, 1950.

Field Hockey

Field Hockey Instructors Guide (2nd ed.). Chicago: The Athletic Institute, 1961.

Lees, Josephine T. and Betty Shellenberger, *Field Hockey for Players, Coaches, and Umpires.* New York: The Ronald Press Company, 1957.

Mackey, Helen T., *Field Hockey: An International Team Sport.* Englewood Cliffs, N.J.: Prentice-Hall, Inc., 1963.

Official Field Hockey–Lacrosse Guide. Washington, D.C.: The Division for Girls and Women's Sports, American Association for Health, Physical Education, and Recreation (published every two years).

Pollard, Marjorie, *Hockey for All.* New York: Thomas Nelson & Sons, 1957.

Selected Field Hockey–Lacrosse Articles. Washington, D.C.: The Division for Girls and Women's Sports, American Association for Health, Physical Education, and Recreation, 1955.

Taylor, Eileen, *Coaching Hockey in Schools.* London: Marjorie Pollard Publications, Ltd., no date.

Townsend, Anne B., *Field Hockey.* New York: Charles Scribner's Sons, 1936.

Lacrosse

Boyd, Margaret, *Lacrosse, Playing and Coaching.* New York: A. S. Barnes & Co., 1959.

Burbeck, Louise G. and Helena Wheeler, *Lacrosse for Girls.* Saratoga, N.Y.: L. G. Burbeck, Skidmore College, no date.

Morrill, W. Kelso, *Lacrosse.* New York: A. S. Barnes & Co., 1952.

Official Field Hockey–Lacrosse Guide. Washington, D.C.: The Division for Girls and Women's Sports, American Association for Health, Physical Education, and Recreation (published every two years).

Selected Field Hockey–Lacrosse Articles. Washington, D.C.: The Division for Girls and Women's Sports, American Association for Health, Physical Education, and Recreation, 1955.

Stanwick, Tad, *Lacrosse.* New York: A. S. Barnes & Co., 1940.

Soccer–Speedball *–Speed-A-Way †

DiClemente, Frank F., *Soccer Illustrated.* New York: A. S. Barnes & Co., 1955.

Fralick, Samuel, *Soccer.* New York: A. S. Barnes & Co., 1945.

Hankinson, J. T. and A. H. Chadder, *Soccer for Schools.* London: George Allen & Unwin, Ltd., 1948.

Hupprich, Florence, *Soccer and Speedball for Girls.* New York: A. S. Barnes & Co., 1942.

Jeffrey, Bill, *The Boys with the Educated Feet.* Minneapolis, Minn.: Burgess Publishing Co., 1938.

Larsen, Marjorie S., *Speed-A-Way, A New Game for Boys and Girls.* Minneapolis, Minn.: Burgess Publishing Co., 1960.

————, *Speed-A-Way.* Stockton, Calif.: Marjorie S. Larsen, 1950.

Mitchell, Elmer D., *Sports for Recreation.* (Speedball) New York: A. S. Barnes & Co., 1952.

Official Soccer–Speedball Guide. Washington, D.C.: The Division for Girls and Women's Sports, American Association for Health, Physical Education, and Recreation (published every two years).

Selected Soccer and Speedball Articles. Washington, D.C.: The Division for Girls and Women's Sports, American Association for Health, Physical Education, and Recreation, 1963.

Soccer Instructors Guide. Chicago: The Athletic Institute, 1961.

V-Five Association of America, *Soccer* (3rd ed.). Annapolis, Md.: United States Naval Institute, 1961.

Winterbottom, Walter, *Training for Soccer.* London: William Heinemann, Ltd., 1960.

————, *Skillful Soccer* (3rd ed.). London: Educational Productions, Ltd., 1956.

---

* A game originated by Elmer D. Mitchell.
† A game originated by Marjorie S. Larsen.

———, *Modern Soccer*. London: Educational Productions, Ltd., 1958.

Softball

Allen, Archie, *Handbook of Baseball Drills*. Englewood Cliffs, N.J.: Prentice-Hall, Inc., 1959.

Baseball Instructors Guide. Chicago: The Athletic Institute, 1958.

Coombs, J. W., *Baseball: Individual Play and Team Strategy* (3rd ed.). Englewood Cliffs, N.J.: Prentice-Hall, Inc., 1951.

DiClemente, Frank F., *Baseball*. Mankato, Minn.: Creative Educational Society, Inc., 1961.

Fischer, Leo H., *How to Play Winning Softball*. Englewood Cliffs, N.J.: Prentice-Hall, Inc., 1940.

Kneer, Marion and Dan Lipinski, *Softball*. New York: Sterling Publishing Co., Inc., 1961.

Lai, William T., *Championship Baseball*. Englewood Cliffs, N.J.: Prentice-Hall, Inc., 1954.

Mitchell, Viola, *Softball for Girls* (3rd ed.). New York: A. S. Barnes & Co., 1952.

Noren, Arthur T., *Softball* (3rd ed.). New York: The Ronald Press Company, 1959.

Official Softball–Track and Field Guide. Washington, D.C.: The Division for Girls and Women's Sports, American Association for Health, Physical Education, and Recreation (published every two years).

Selected Softball Articles. Washington, D.C.: The Division for Girls and Women's Sports, American Association for Health, Physical Education, and Recreation (current edition).

Softball Instructors Guide. Chicago: The Athletic Institute, 1953.

Spackman, Robert Jr., *Baseball*. Annapolis, Md.: United States Naval Institute, 1963.

Touch Football

Allen, George, *Complete Book of Winning Football Drills*. Englewood Cliffs, N.J.: Prentice-Hall, Inc., 1959.

Barbour, R. H. and L. Savia, *Touch Football*. New York: Appleton-Century-Crofts, Inc., 1933.

Bateman, John F. and Paul V. Governali, *Football Fundamentals*. New York: McGraw-Hill Book Company, 1957.

Cox, William R., *Better Football for Boys*. New York: Dodd, Mead & Co., 1958.

Duncan, Ray O., *Six-Man Football*. New York: A. S. Barnes & Co., 1940.

Epler, Stephen, *Six-Man Football*. New York: Harper & Row, Publishers, 1938.

Grombach, J. V., *Touch Football*. New York: A. S. Barnes & Co., 1942.

Otto, J. R., *Football*. Mankato, Minn.: Creative Educational Society, Inc., 1961.

Stanbury, Dean and Frank DeSantis, *Touch Football*. New York: Sterling Publishing Co., Inc., 1961.

V-Five Association of America, *Football* (2nd ed.). Annapolis, Md.: United States Naval Institute, 1950.

Volleyball

Brownell, Clifford L. and Roy H. Moore, *Recreational Sports*. Mankato, Minn.: Creative Educational Society, Inc., 1961.

Brumbach, Wayne B., *Beginning Volleyball*. Eugene, Ore.: The University of Oregon Cooperative Store, 1961.

Emery, Curtis R., *Modern Volleyball*. New York: The Macmillan Company, 1953.

Laveaga, Robert E., *Volleyball* (2nd ed.). New York: The Ronald Press Company, 1960.

Odeneal, William T. and Harry E. Wilson, *Beginning Volleyball*. Belmont, Calif.: Wadsworth Publishing Company, Inc., 1962.

Official Recreational Games–Volleyball Guide. Washington, D.C.: The Division for Girls and Women's Sports, American Association for Health, Physical Education, and Recreation (published every two years).

Official Volleyball Rules and Reference Guide. Berne, Ind.: United States Volleyball Association, 1962.

Selected Volleyball Articles. Washington, D.C.: The Division for Girls and Women's Sports, American Association for Health, Physical Education, and Recreation, 1959.

U.S. Volleyball Association Guide. American Sports Publishing Company, 1957.

Volleyball Instructors Guide. Chicago: The Athletic Institute, 1961.

Welch, J. Edmund, ed., *How to Play and Teach Volleyball*. New York: Association Press, 1960.

Games

Bancroft, Jessie, *Games* (rev. ed.). New York: The Macmillan Company, 1952.

Donnelly, Richard J., William G. Helms, and Elmer D. Mitchell, *Active Games and Contests* (2nd ed.). New York: The Ronald Press Company, 1958.

Gilb, Stella, *Games for the Gymnasium, Playground and Classroom*. Lexington, Ky.: Hurst Printing Co., 1954.

Hindman, Darwin A., *Handbook of Active Games*. Englewood Cliffs, N.J.: Prentice-Hall, Inc., 1951.

Latchaw, Marjorie, *A Pocket Guide of Games and Rhythms for the Elementary School*. Englewood Cliffs, N.J.: Prentice-Hall, Inc., 1956.

Richardson, Hazel, *Games for the Elementary School Grades*. Minneapolis, Minn.: Burgess Publishing Company, 1958.

————, *Games for Junior and Senior High Schools*. Minneapolis, Minn.: Burgess Publishing Company, 1957.

Riley, Marie, *Secondary and Lead-up Games Card File*. Cortland, N.Y.: State University Teachers College Book Store, 1959.